Modernizing China
Post-Mao Reform and Development

Also of Interest

†*The Making of Foreign Policy in China: Structure and Process*, A. Doak Barnett

China on the Eve of Communist Takeover, A. Doak Barnett

†*The Government and Politics of the PRC: A Time of Transition*, Jürgen Domes

Six Chapters of Life in a Cadre School: Memoirs from China's Cultural Revolution, Yang Chiang, Translated and Annotated by Djang Chu

Revolution in China, C. P. Fitzgerald

China: A Short Cultural History, C. P. Fitzgerald

Human Rights in Post-Mao China, John Copper, Franz Michael, and Yuan-li Wu

†*China Briefing, 1984*, edited by Steven M. Goldstein

Perspectives on Development in Mainland China, edited by King-yuh Chang

Mainland China: Politics, Economics, and Reform, edited by Yu-ming Shaw

Power and Policy in the PRC, edited by Yu-ming Shaw

China's Political/Military Evolution: The Party and the Military in the PRC, 1960–1984, Monte R. Bullard

Partnership with China: Sino-Foreign Joint Ventures in Historical Perspective, David G. Brown

†*China Through the Ages*, Franz Michael

†Available in hardcover and paperback.

About the Book and Editors

Since the death of Mao, China has entered a new period in its development. Turning away from the all-encompassing emphasis on revolutionary struggle and ideological transformation that characterized the last years of the Maoist era, China's leaders under Deng Xiaoping have initiated dramatic new reform and development policies. In original essays, the contributors, all senior specialists on contemporary China, analyze the reasons for the new policies, the nature and impact of the changes now occurring, and the prospects for a continuation of these policies in the future. Specifically, they examine the Chinese polity as a "consultative authoritarian" system, the far-reaching changes in China's agriculture, important shifts in foreign economic relations, the gradual modernization policy pursued by its military leaders, the relaxation of controls on cultural life, and the possibility that current social policies may well increase equality rather than inequality in Chinese society.

The authors conclude that it is too early to judge the eventual, long-term outcome of current reforms, which they believe grew out of the political crises and chronic economic problems that afflicted China in the late 1960s and early 1970s. Although they see some opposition and built-in limits to reform, on balance they foresee strong support for continued reform and believe it will be difficult for future leaders to reverse course.

A. Doak Barnett is professor of Chinese Studies at the School of Advanced International Studies, The Johns Hopkins University. His books include *Uncertain Passage: China's Transition to the Post-Mao Era*, *China on the Eve of Communist Takeover* (reissued by Westview), and *The Making of Foreign Policy in China: Structure and Process* (Westview). **Ralph N. Clough** is coordinator of the SAIS China Forum at the School of Advanced International Studies, The Johns Hopkins University. His books include *East Asia and U.S. Security* and *Island China*.

Publication of
SAIS China Forum
Edwin O. Reischauer Center for East Asian Studies
School of Advanced International Studies
The Johns Hopkins University

Modernizing China
Post-Mao Reform and Development

edited by
A. Doak Barnett and
Ralph N. Clough

Westview Press / Boulder and London

Copyright © 1986 by The Johns Hopkins University

Published in 1986 in the United States of America by Westview Press, Inc.; Frederick A. Praeger, Publisher; 5500 Central Avenue, Boulder, Colorado 80301

Library of Congress Cataloging in Publication Data
Main entry under title:
Modernizing China.
   Includes index.
   1. China—Politics and government—1976–
2. China—Social conditions—1976–   . I. Barnett,
A. Doak. II. Clough, Ralph N., 1916–
DS779.26.M63 1986   951.05′7   85-17982
ISBN 0-8133-0332-X
ISBN 0-8133-0333-8 (pbk.)

Printed and bound in the United States of America

10   9   8   7   6   5   4   3   2   1

Contents

Tables

Preface

The SAIS China Forum was established in 1984, at The Johns Hopkins School of Advanced International Studies, to organize lectures, symposia, seminars, and other programs focused on China and U.S.-China relations. A part of the Edwin O. Reischauer Center for East Asian Studies at SAIS, the Forum brings together a wide range of distinguished scholars, diplomats, civil servants, businesspeople, and others to examine major trends and developments, as well as key problems and issues, relating to China and U.S. policy toward China. The majority of the meetings it sponsors are open not only to SAIS faculty and students but also to others in the Washington, D.C., area who are seriously interested in these subjects.

During the academic year 1984-1985, the SAIS China Forum organized a major series of lectures by leading American scholars on "China's Modernization." These lectures, subsequently revised, are the basis for this volume. Each of the five authors is a recognized leader in his discipline and area of special expertise in the broad field of China studies: Dwight Perkins, of Harvard University, in economics; Harry Harding, of the Brookings Institution, in politics; Paul H.B. Godwin, of the Air University, in military affairs; Perry Link, of the University of California at Los Angeles, in literature; and Martin King Whyte, of the University of Michigan, in sociology. The Forum asked the authors to give their analyses and interpretations of the most significant changes that have occurred in China since the death of Mao in different sectors of society—which are indicated by the chapter titles—and to present their views succinctly and in a form that would be aimed not only at other scholars and students of China but also at the "informed public" with interests in China. We believe they have succeeded admirably and that this small volume should be of wide interest because it gives the considered judgments of individuals who are among the best qualified anywhere to give such judgments on the extraordinary processes of change that have been unleashed in China during the past eight years, as well as on the likely consequences of these changes in the years ahead.

The coeditors express their gratitude first of all to the five authors. They also wish to express their great appreciation to Benjamin T. Rome, whose financial support made possible the SAIS China Forum programs that resulted in this book, and to Barbara S. Bowersox, Program Coordinator, who assisted at every stage in organizing SAIS China Forum programs and producing this book. Additional thanks are due those at Westview Press who made possible the rapid copyediting and publication of the book—in particular, Senior Editor Libby Barstow and Copy Editor Christine Arden.

A. Doak Barnett
Ralph N. Clough
Washington, D.C.

Introduction

A. Doak Barnett
Ralph N. Clough

Since Mao Zedong's death in 1976, China has entered a very new period in its history—a period best described as one of reform and development. Turning away from the emphasis on revolutionary struggle and ideological transformation that characterized the last years of the Maoist era, China's post-Mao leaders, under the slogan of "Four Modernizations," now stress political stability and economic development rather than ideological struggle and class conflict. Pragmatic adaptation of policy to solve pressing concrete problems has replaced utopian efforts to transform society in the name of egalitarian goals.

The drive to achieve "Four Modernizations" by the end of this century calls for far-reaching changes in China's agriculture, industry, national defense, and science and technology. Zhou Enlai first articulated the general goal of modernizing China in these four areas in the mid-1960s and then again in the mid-1970s, but opposition from China's radicals prevented any basic policy shifts until after Mao's death. Major changes began when Deng Xiaoping emerged as the dominant figure in China's leadership in late 1978; the introduction of sweeping reform policies accelerated thereafter, especially after Deng had consolidated his political position during the period 1978–1981; and these reforms have been steadily broadened ever since then.

Some of the policies that have emerged since 1978 have roots in three earlier periods, especially 1956–1957, 1961–1962, and 1974–1975. Deng Xiaoping was in the forefront of those leaders favoring increased pragmatism throughout the 1960s and 1970s, as a consequence of which he was twice purged by Mao. As long as Mao lived, all efforts to shift in any major way from revolution to reform were aborted either by Mao himself or by radicals closely associated with him.

Since Mao's death, the purge of China's leading radicals, and Deng's achievement of primacy in the leadership, however, the shifts in policy

1

have been very dramatic, going far beyond what most observers would have considered possible prior to 1976. They are clearly changing the nature of the political, economic, and social systems in China in significant ways.

The authors of this book were asked to determine what the most important changes have been in five critical areas and to analyze not only what the new policies are but also the reasons for their adoption and their impact on China to date. In addition, the authors were requested to provide informed judgments on the likely consequences and prospects for success of these new policies in the years immediately ahead.

All of the authors are impressed by the degree of change that has already occurred in China, but they also make it clear that China's leaders will face major problems and obstacles as they continue in their attempts to alter China's political system, economy, military establishment, cultural life, and social structure. The situations and the prospects are by no means identical throughout the five areas discussed; nevertheless, the overall picture that emerges suggests that very far-reaching, even historic, transformations may now be altering the nature of the political and economic systems and of society at large. Although cautious in making specific predictions, the authors believe that, at least in the foreseeable future, China is not likely to turn back—either toward policies similar to those of the 1950s, when Chinese leaders regarded the Soviet Union as their model, or toward policies of revolutionary radicalism, comparable to those of the late Maoist era. However, the authors also believe that it is too early to judge exactly how far China will go down its present path.

In his analysis in Chapter 1 of China's political development in the post-Mao period, Harry Harding argues that recent reform policies in the political system can be understood only if one recognizes that at the end of the Maoist era the country faced a severe political crisis. China at that time, he asserts, represented a case of "decayed totalitarianism," and the steps taken since Mao's death in response to the crises of the 1960s and 1970s have resulted in very significant changes in the political system.

Harding discusses a wide variety of political reforms introduced in recent years, aimed at redefining the relationship of state and society, revitalizing all governing institutions, altering relationships between the Communist party and other political hierarchies, restoring unity and broadening the consensus within the leadership, preparing for an orderly succession, and changing the basis for political authority and legitimacy in China. Specific reforms already implemented have, in varying ways and degrees, reduced party intervention in ordinary lives, allowed greater freedom of intellectual life, begun to build a legal system, widened grass-roots political participation, shaken up the regime's administrative bureaucracies, and altered personnel policies so as to put new emphasis on youth, education, and skills in recruitment of people for the bureaucracies and in promotion to posts of leadership.

Important achievements have clearly been made in all of these areas, as Harding notes, but opposition to change persists (coming more from conservatives, he believes, than from radicals), and there are limits to how far even the reformers are prepared to go. Harding labels the Chinese polity today a "consultative authoritarian" system, falling somewhere between the totalitarianism of the past and a fully democratic system. A key question now, he asserts, is how far "liberalization" will go. He believes that, although the "consultative aspects" of the system may continue to expand, the demands for more far-reaching liberalization are likely to be relatively weak, and conservative opposition to further liberalization may be strong. China, he concludes, is not likely to develop genuine pluralism, with autonomous organizations contesting for political power. In light of China's authoritarian traditions, this conclusion is perhaps not surprising.

The relationship between political and economic changes in post-Mao China is a complex one. The two areas are obviously linked, yet the extent of reform in one area seems likely to differ from that in the other. Clearly, a basic political shift had to occur before economic reform policies could be adopted. However, China's post-Mao leaders will probably be prepared to go even further in reforming the economic system than in altering the political system.

Dwight Perkins, in Chapter 2, analyzes what he describes as "seven years of uninterrupted efforts at economic reform," in which China has departed in very important ways from the Soviet-style system it had adopted in the 1950s. He focuses attention both on the causes of reform and on the prospects in the period ahead. In contrast to Harding's analysis, which maintains that China experienced a severe political crisis at the end of the Maoist era that set in motion the process of political reform, Perkins argues that what triggered the post-Mao economic reforms was not an acute short-term crisis in the economy but, rather, chronic long-term problems that could not be solved without fundamental changes in the system. The Cultural Revolution did, at the start, have adverse effects on the economy, but, as Perkins points out, growth resumed soon thereafter and, overall, both agriculture and industry achieved growth rates that were quite respectable during the final decade of the Maoist era. However, the growth rates were very deceptive, Perkins emphasizes, because the growth that was achieved required extremely high rates of investment, involved great waste and inefficiency, was plagued by serious bottle-necks, and failed to improve in any significant way the living standards of most ordinary Chinese. According to Perkins, it was in response to these chronic problems—although not necessarily with any very clear understanding of them at the start—that Chinese leaders began to introduce economic reforms soon after Mao's death.

Perkins outlines the most important policy changes aimed at reform. One important move was the decision to end China's isolation and expand foreign economic relations—by developing international trade, importing technology, promoting exports, training Chinese in the West, borrowing abroad, encouraging foreign investments in China, and establishing special economic zones in several sectors to stimulate trade and investment. Another basic, far-reaching decision was to try to improve economic incentives throughout the economy.

The most dramatic reforms to date, Perkins points out, have been those in agriculture—especially the adoption of the "responsibility system" based on household contracts, which, for all practical purposes, has ended agricultural collectivization and has been a major factor boosting farm output to new highs. Urban and industrial reforms, which aim at increasing enterprise autonomy, reducing central planning, and expanding the role of market forces, are still in their early stages and have a long way to go to be effective.

Perkins asks, as does Harding, how far the reforms—in particular, urban industrial reforms—are likely to go, and what further steps would be required to alter the basic nature of the economic system in China. If the program of urban and industrial reforms announced by the Central Committee in October 1984 is to be implemented effectively, Perkins argues, certain major changes must be brought about so as to ensure, first, that the necessary inputs into production are available on the market; second, that enterprise managers will respond to market signals; third, that prices are realistic and reflective of relative scarcities; and, fourth, that there is real competition among economic enterprises. Perkins emphasizes that each of these changes is complex; moreover, all are interrelated, and they must be introduced in tandem.

In light of the changes made so far and the unavoidable difficulties that lie ahead, how, in general, should one assess the prospects for economic reform in China? Perkins believes that because the agricultural reforms have benefited a large majority of China's rural population and have contributed to the remarkable successes in agricultural growth, it would be difficult for future leaders to try to reverse the rural reforms—especially the household contract system. In the industrial sector, progress has been slower than that in the agricultural sector and resistance to reform has been greater; nevertheless, Perkins believes, there is now some "built-in momentum toward reform," even in the industrial sector. Overall, therefore, he judges that economic reform is not simply "a slender reed"; neither, however, is it yet "unstoppable." In his judgment, it is still too early to know "whether China's economic system will retain the key features of the Soviet command model or will evolve into something quite different." The outcome will be determined, he believes, by events during the second half of the 1980s.

Perkins is cautious in predicting how far economic reform will go, and his caution is certainly justified. Yet, it is significant that he believes there is important support for continuing reforms; that the agricultural reforms have already reached the point where any reversal would be difficult and is therefore unlikely; and that, despite all problems and resistances, there is momentum toward further urban and industrial reforms.

Any serious examination of overall trends in China must include an analysis not only of the polity and economy but also of the trends affecting the military establishment. Throughout the modern period, military leaders and forces have played critically important roles in China's development—and they have been greatly influenced, in turn, by general political and economic trends.

In his discussion of the Chinese "defense establishment in transition" in Chapter 3, Paul Godwin focuses his attention on military modernization as one of China's "Four Modernizations," rather than on the changing political and economic roles of the People's Liberation Army (PLA). His analysis of reforms in the military establishment thus complements Harding's analysis of political reforms and the analysis by Perkins of economic reforms.

Godwin's discussion makes it clear that current Chinese defense modernization policies parallel and reflect the overall thrust toward realism, pragmatism, and moderation in the political and economic spheres. In abandoning old dogmas rooted in China's revolutionary past, China's military leaders are now "modernizing" the PLA's doctrine and training as well as its equipment. Moreover, as Godwin notes, instead of basing defense policies on short-term considerations, the Chinese view the task of modernizing their defense establishment essentially as one part of the broad, long-term process of overall national development in China.

Currently, military modernization rates fourth among the "Four Modernizations" as an investment priority. According to Godwin, the Chinese see no immediate military threat requiring a huge short-term increase in investments in the armed forces; in addition, they recognize that at present they could not, in any case, effectively absorb massive infusions of new military technology. With limited resources, they are therefore attempting, incrementally, to improve the combat effectiveness of their existing forces; but their primary aim, in Godwin's view, is gradually to develop, over the very long run, solid foundations for a defense establishment that can both create and sustain modern forces—without any dependence on external technology or supply. Toward this end, they are now stressing in particular both the need to improve the training and structure of the officer corps and the need to redefine military doctrine and strategy under the slogan "People's War Under Modern Conditions."

The long-term Chinese goal requires the creation of a broad modern industrial base to produce up-to-date military equipment, rather than large-scale importation of such equipment. Although the Chinese will import selected defense technology, Godwin says, their primary stress will be on the development of China's own capabilities. The Chinese recognize that this development calls for broad-based civilian as well as military-related industries and also for increasing cooperation between the civilian and military industrial sectors, rather than a crash program giving priority to military modernization.

Godwin maintains that even though major debates have occurred over defense modernization policy, and although there is still some opposition to certain reforms—especially, perhaps, those aimed at reforming the officer corps—Chinese leaders are now confident that over the long run they will be able to build a technological and industrial base capable of sustaining modern forces independently. Moreover, although the current situation is a transitional one, in which policy aims at overcoming military weaknesses only gradually, Godwin argues that China's military elite now "knows where it wants to go." He also asserts that, by the end of the century, China will have reduced the "gross disparity" between itself and other major powers, and that China's military establishment will be very different from what it is today—"if the current pattern of defense modernization endures." He does not state explicitly whether he thinks the pattern will endure, but the general thrust of his analysis suggests that he believes it will.

In China, although the military establishment has frequently played extremely important political and social roles (in fact if not in theory), the country's ideal has been rule by an educated elite. China's bureaucracies traditionally were staffed mainly by civilian scholar-bureaucrats, who enjoyed much higher status than military men. In the modern period, intellectuals have carried on this tradition in some respects, and, even though they have seldom exercised great political power directly, they have exerted an influence on political leaders, and on the society as a whole, disproportionate to their numbers.

During the Communists' rise to power, intellectuals under party leadership played a crucial role in mobilizing mass support, especially in the countryside. However, after achieving power, the party imposed tight controls over intellectual life, and over time these controls alienated a large portion of China's intellectuals. Attacks on intellectuals during the "Anti-Rightist" campaign in 1957, and then even broader attacks on them after the start of the Cultural Revolution in 1966, suppressed almost all independent thought and demoralized a large percentage of China's intellectuals.

Under Deng Xiaoping, China's reform leaders have recognized the importance of relaxing controls, raising the status of intellectuals, encouraging their creativity, and mobilizing their talents—especially those of China's scientific and technical experts but also those of writers and other intellectuals—to support China's modernization.

Perry Link, in his chapter on cultural policy under the Deng regime, concentrates his attention on China's writers—members of a literary elite that, while small, is nevertheless very influential. After discussing the centuries-old ties between literature and politics—and the traditional view of Chinese writers that they should concern themselves with political and social issues, and that political leaders should heed their views—Link asserts that the most important "cultural reform" in China in the post-Mao period has been the "dramatic relaxation of controls on cultural expression."

In discussing why China's post-Mao reform leaders decided to relax controls, Link indicates that he believes they did so to heal wounds inflicted in the past, to win popular support for the present regime, and to obtain the cooperation of intellectuals that leaders recognize is essential to their overall modernization policies—especially the cooperation of scientists, engineers, and educated youth. Link speculates that another factor was the desire to make a good impression on foreigners. He also maintains that at least some of China's current leaders regard cultural creativity as an important feature of "enlightened Marxism."

Whatever the motivations, the effects described by Link have been quite far reaching. The status and working conditions of writers have improved, a major revival of interest in both traditional Chinese culture and foreign culture has occurred, and the scope for creativity for Chinese writers has been greatly broadened. Link also notes the occurrence of certain modernist experiments in recent Chinese literature (for example, writing in which individuals turn inward to explore the psyche, and experiments in "stream-of-consciousness" writing) and discusses the strong opposition expressed within the literary community itself against such trends because they appear to conflict with important traditional Chinese values.

Link further indicates that no group of dissidents comparable to that in the Soviet Union has emerged in China, despite the cultural thaw. He believes several factors help to explain this fact, including the existence of more effective psychological controls on writers in China, the weakness of ties between Chinese writers and potential supporters abroad, and, perhaps most important, the deep traditions that strongly predispose Chinese intellectuals against any action that might involve even the appearance of disloyalty to China.

Like the authors of earlier chapters, Link not only examines the nature and extent of recent reforms but also gives his views on their limits and potential for reversibility. His basic judgments are very similar in important respects to those made by the other contributors about political and economic reforms. There clearly are "outer limits" to the freedom that will be granted to writers, he believes, and there is little prospect that the Communist party will abandon or lose its right to impose such limits. He notes that at times the trend toward relaxation of controls in the post-Mao era has been interrupted by periodic moves to tighten controls somewhat—but he also points out that each of these "temporary contractions" has been followed by renewed steps toward relaxation. Link asserts that, in his judgment, cultural policy is inherently more volatile, and more reversible, than many other kinds of policy in China. Nevertheless, on balance, he believes not only that "no fact [in the cultural field] is as basic as the major general relaxation" of controls but also that the relaxation deserves to be called "dramatic." Although he does not rule out the possibility of a return to tighter controls, Link believes that the support of the current and emerging leaders in China for the relaxation of controls on intellectuals means that any return to a "totalitarian cultural policy" would be difficult.

The fundamental shift in the leadership's general outlook and priorities in post-Mao China and the leaders' determination to reform all aspects of society have meant that this has been a period not only of rapid policy changes affecting the political, economic, military, and cultural spheres but a period of broad social change as well.

In Chapter 5, Martin Whyte examines post-Mao social trends not by trying to summarize all of the trends now under way but by focusing on one key issue: the relationship between economic development and equality and inequality in Chinese society. He begins by noting that the conventional wisdom has been that Mao, in his last years, saw a basic conflict between egalitarian goals and economic development and decided to subordinate development to egalitarianism, whereas China's post-Mao leaders, predisposed to move in the opposite direction, have been determined to give priority to economic development, even if it results in more inequality—at least in the short run.

Whyte discusses the rhetoric, as well as the facts, on which this conventional wisdom has been based, but he then argues that, in fact, China was less egalitarian in the Maoist period than is commonly assumed, and that trends in the post-Mao era, while complex, are not necessarily increasing the degree of inequality in Chinese society. On the contrary, they may actually be resulting in greater equality overall.

Whyte maintains that to judge equality and inequality in any society, one ideally should examine a wide variety of indicators or measures relating to economic position (including measures of income, consumption, and property), political powers (including judgments—if not measures—about different individuals' and groups' rights and privileges, and changes in the broad relationship between state and society), and social status (including measures not only of stratification but also of social mobility). Moreover, he emphasizes, it is necessary to recognize that trends affecting equality and inequality may differ among subunits of a nation or society. Whyte acknowledges that the data available on China are insufficient to reach firm conclusions on trends affecting all those factors that determine equality or inequality, but he believes that some tentative conclusions about trends in both the late Mao and post-Mao periods can be drawn.

In reexamining the trends in the last years of the Maoist era, Whyte concludes that, although income differentials at that time probably decreased within local units (that is, in cities, or in rural production units), the urban-rural gap seemed to grow, and differences between different rural areas also appeared to increase. Moreover, it is his view that, despite increased mass participation in politics in the late Maoist period, political inequalities grew as a result of growing political struggles, class discrimination, and the labeling of sizable numbers of people as political pariahs. He also argues that, after the peak of the Cultural Revolution had been reached, China's reconstructed bureaucracies became even more dominant than they had been in the past.

Whyte maintains that despite the leadership's post-Mao denunciation of egalitarianism and encouragement of material incentives that tend to widen income differentials, one cannot assume that inequalities in China are now actually increasing overall. There are conflicting trends affecting the urban-rural gap, he believes, but, on balance, the results may be arresting the previous widening of the urban-rural gap—and, in fact, may actually be narrowing it. The data relevant to other regional differences are inconclusive in his view, but here too there are conflicting trends, at least some of which have had the effect of reducing regional inequalities. Accordingly, Whyte speculates that while inequalities in local areas have been increasing, the urban-rural gap may have been narrowing somewhat, and that the trends affecting other regional inequalities are mixed and difficult to judge.

Whyte is inclined to be cautiously optimistic about the prospect that the post-Mao reform policies will not, on the whole, lead to greater income inequality. He argues that one should not assume that state redistribution always fosters economic equality or that market relationships inevitably foster inequality, and that, despite the skepticism of many about the idea that the benefits of economic growth will "trickle down" in China, this *could* happen—and might well result in greater equality (as it has in some other developing countries and areas in Asia).

In the distribution of power in post-Mao China, the overall trend, in Whyte's judgment, has doubtless been toward greater equality; compared with the past, the state is now less intrusive, individuals and social groups have more autonomy, discriminatory class labels have been removed from millions of individuals, a legal system is gradually developing, and new constraints have been imposed on bureaucrats—all of which, he believes, tend to reduce political inequalities.

Although the five authors in this book focus their attention on changes in different sectors of Chinese society, and although their judgments vary in certain respects, what is striking is the broad area of consensus among them. All five believe that very profound, far-reaching changes are occurring in post-Mao China and that the effects of the reform and development processes under way are changing China's basic political, economic, and social systems. All tend to view favorably the reforms that have been adopted, as well as most of the actual changes that have taken place to date. In general, moreover, they all tend to be optimistic about the likelihood that current policies and the general directions of change will continue; none completely rules out the possibility of a reversal of policy direction, but all now see this as unlikely.

However, although all five authors are reasonably confident that processes of reform and development now under way will continue (at least for some time) in the current general directions, they are uncertain as to how far these processes will go. They all see some opposition to current trends, and they all believe that various factors— including tradition and the intrinsic problems of reform—will impose some limits on the development of current trends. But exactly where China will be by the end of the century on the political spectrum, between totalitarianism and pluralism—or on the economic spectrum, between a Soviet-style command system and "market socialism" of some kind—is still, they believe, unpredictable. The answers to these questions will emerge only gradually as processes of reform and development in China unfold. Although the authors of this book avoid clear prognostications about the likely end results of current policies (and they are wise not to try to predict the unpredictable), they nevertheless give us a clear picture of the directions in which China is now moving and of the key changes we should watch for in the years ahead as future events begin to answer questions that are not now answerable.

1
Political Development in Post-Mao China

Harry Harding

Of all the reforms that have swept China since the death of Mao Zedong in 1976, those in the economic realm have attracted the greatest attention abroad. The transformation of the economic systems—first of rural and then of urban China—has aroused vigorous debate among Western observers over whether China has adopted capitalism, instituted a market economy, or merely modified the ways in which a socialist system is planned and managed. Less noted, but equally significant, have been the changes in the political institutions that govern China's 1 billion people. Here, too, one can usefully ask whether China has moved toward a more liberal, pragmatic, and pluralistic political order, or whether it has simply become a routinized authoritarian system similar to the post-Stalinist Soviet Union.

The issue arises because the political evolution of post-Mao China has been riddled with contradictions. Political participation has expanded substantially, but strict limits remain on both the form and the content of political expression. Although the last decade has witnessed an erosion of the role of ideology in political and intellectual affairs, periodic campaigns have been launched against "bourgeois liberalism," "spiritual pollution," "ultraleftism," and other ideas officially defined as heterodox. Chinese leaders have placed heavy emphasis on the development of regular bureaucratic procedures and institutional processes, but they have also implemented their reforms through a party rectification campaign reminiscent of the original *zhengfeng* movement in Yan'an as well as through a restaffing of the bureaucracy comparable in scale, although not in method, to the

For comments on an earlier draft of this chapter, I am grateful to Doak Barnett, Ralph Clough, Bruce Dickson, Constance Squires-Meaney, and Andrew Walder.

Cultural Revolution. An understanding of the political development of China in the post-Mao period requires that we give attention to both aspects of these contradictions in an attempt to assess the relative balance between them.

Decayed Totalitarianism

In Chapter 2, Dwight Perkins suggests that China did not experience an acute economic crisis in 1976 but was facing instead the more subtle and chronic problems of low efficiency and restricted consumption. Economic reform in such a circumstance may be highly desirable, but, as the experience of the Soviet Union has demonstrated for so long, it is hardly inevitable.

Chinese politics, in contrast, presented a quite different situation. The Chinese political system at the time of Mao's death had a dual character. It was, on the one hand, a totalitarian system with the capability to penetrate and at least partially control all areas of social, economic, and political life. And yet, on the other hand, it was also a system in serious decay. As a result of the Cultural Revolution, it had lost a large measure of its organizational vigor, its elite unity, and its popular support. This combination of totalitarianism and decay was so unstable that it virtually compelled some kind of political reform immediately upon the death of Mao Zedong.

The totalitarianism of China at the end of Mao's life was similar in many ways to the totalitarianism that existed in the Soviet Union under Stalin.[1] Both Maoism and Stalinism reflected an attempt to achieve complete penetration and control of society and to eliminate any islands of exemption, no matter how trivial, from political intervention. Both systems justified these controls in the name of a sweeping socioeconomic transformation of society that they described as just and progressive. Both systems imposed an arbitrary reign of terror against "class enemies"—often defined on the basis of class background, political orientation, or occupation—who allegedly resisted this revolutionary change. Both Mao and Stalin emerged as charismatic leaders, casting aside established party policymaking institutions in favor of their own personal rule, assisted by impermanent and unstable groups of courtiers and favorites.

Taken by themselves, these aspects of totalitarianism were probably destined to lead to substantial change in China after Mao's death, comparable perhaps to the process of de-Stalinization that occurred in the Soviet Union after 1956, as both the bureaucratic elite and the general public pressed for greater predictability in politics and greater freedom in social affairs. But in China the impetus for change was intensified by the second characteristic of politics in the late Mao period: its serious decay and instability. It is this second factor that explains why China faced an even more serious political crisis at the time of Mao's death than did the Soviet Union upon the death of Stalin.

If the totalitarian characteristics of Chinese politics in the mid-1970s reflected the similarities between Maoism and Stalinism, the decay of Chinese political institutions between 1966 and 1976 stemmed from the differences between the two political movements. In short, Stalinist totalitarianism was fundamentally conservative and elitist and thus created relatively stable political institutions, whereas the Maoist variant was radical and populist and tended therefore to undermine political stability.

More specifically, Stalin encouraged the decline of utopian thought and its replacement by a more conservative nationalism; in contrast, Maoism attempted to revive revolutionary ideology and to implement radical socioeconomic policies. Thus, where Stalin encouraged the emergence of inequalities in status and income in the name of modernization, Mao favored a greater degree of egalitarianism in the name of continued revolution. Stalin's purges removed veteran revolutionaries in favor of younger technocrats, whereas Mao's Cultural Revolution aimed to rid the party and state bureaucracies of veteran specialists and to replace them with younger revolutionaries. Most important of all, Stalinist terror was state terror, carried out under the control of a dictator through the state security apparatus. In contrast, Maoist terror, at least at the height of the Cultural Revolution, was mass terror, imposed by loosely organized Red Guard groups only partially controlled by Mao and his lieutenants.

It was these aspects of Maoism that produced the political decay of the mid-1970s. First, the Maoist preference for "redness" over "expertise," and the insistence on maintaining the "purity of class ranks," meant that recruitment to Communist party membership and to cadre positions within the party came to be based on class background and political loyalty rather than on technical training or administrative competence. At the same time, the Maoist disdain for regularized personnel procedures meant that appointments to official positions were without fixed term, subject to removal only by death, promotion, or political purge. The result was a bureaucracy that, by the mid-1970s, was woefully overaged and underskilled.

Second, during the Cultural Revolution, Mao mobilized the "masses" of urban China, particularly high-school and university students, to attack "capitalist roaders" in the party and government. But, in so doing, he stripped legitimacy from established institutions without creating any alternative organizational form for channeling the new waves of participation that he had unleashed. The result, to borrow Samuel Huntington's classic formulation, was that participation increased as the level of institutionalization decreased, thus leading to political instability approaching chaos from the fall of 1966 to the fall of 1968.[2]

At this point, Mao recognized the need to hold China together, but he was not prepared completely to repudiate the Cultural Revolution he had launched. Accordingly, he resorted to a series of half-measures after 1967 that ended most mass disorder but perpetuated the political decay at higher levels. He called in the army to restore order, allowed military officers to assume key positions in the party and state bureaucracies, and named the defense minister, Lin Biao, as his presumptive successor. But within two years, when Mao came to suspect that the military's involvement in civilian matters might become permanent, he launched a series of maneuvers to dislodge Lin from party leadership and to reduce the role of the PLA in civilian political life. In similar fashion, Mao sponsored the political rehabilitation of many of the victims of the Cultural Revolution in the early 1970s. But he did not permit a systematic purge of the leftists who had risen to power during the course of the movement, and he even encouraged the leftists to continue to portray the victims of the Cultural Revolution as "unrepentant capitalist roaders." As a result of Mao's ambivalence, the process of rebuilding the political system was bogged down in intense factional conflict, first between civilian cadres and military officers, and then between radicals and moderates.

This period of protracted stalemate, extending from the suppression of the Red Guard movement in 1968 to the purge of the Gang of Four after Mao's death in 1976, produced the final and most serious aspect of political decay: a severe crisis of confidence among important sectors of Chinese society, particularly intellectuals and urban youth. The crisis reflected the widespread disgust at organizational inefficiency and leadership factionalism, the anger of intellectuals at the persecution they suffered at the hands of the radicals, and the sense of betrayal among young people who had been encouraged to join the Red Guards but who were then dispatched to the countryside when their movement became unruly. The loss of confidence in the regime was exemplified by the Tiananmen Incident of April 1976, in which hundreds of thousands of people in Peking participated in an unauthorized memorial tribute to Zhou Enlai, who to them was a symbol of a more humane and stable political process.

The political crisis confronting China at the time of Mao's death led a group of reformers, under the leadership of Deng Xiaoping, to conclude that political change was both essential and urgent. There has been no precise blueprint for the reforms, and they have evolved gradually and somewhat sporadically since 1977.[3] Nonetheless, a retrospective examination of the evolution of Chinese politics over the last eight years suggests that the reforms fall into five broad categories: (1) encouragement of a reconciliation between the party and society by reducing the scope and arbitrariness of political intervention in daily life; (2) expansion of opportunities for popular participation in political affairs, albeit with limits on both the form and content of political expression; (3) efforts to revitalize all institutions of governance, by restaffing them with younger and better-educated officials, and by granting them greater autonomy from party control; (4) measures to restore normalcy and unity to elite politics, so as to bring to an end the chronic instability of the late Maoist period and to create a more orderly process of leadership succession; and (5) steps to redefine the content and role of China's official ideology, so as to create a new basis for authority in contemporary Chinese politics.

As we shall see, impressive achievements have been scored in each of these areas. The result has been that Chinese politics today is much more institutionalized, much less decayed, and much less totalitarian than it was in 1976. In that sense, the immediate political crisis engendered by the late Maoist period has been resolved. And yet there have been limits on what has been sought, and what has been achieved, in all five aspects of reform. As a consequence, although China has passed from totalitarianism into a form of consultative authoritarianism, it has not yet become a truly pluralistic political order. The issue for the future is whether social and economic modernization will create pressures for further liberalization that, in turn, may produce another crisis of political development in post-Mao China.

Reconciliation Between Party and Society

The most pressing political problem to be addressed in the post-Mao period was the alienation of large sectors of urban China from the leadership of the Communist party as a result of the totalitarian features of the late Maoist period. The reconciliation forged between party and society has involved a series of measures designed to reduce the scope and arbitrariness of political intervention in social life.

The reduction of the scope of political interference in society has been evident in artistic matters, intellectual affairs, and daily life. In the arts, the authorities now allow greater room for creative expression; indeed, they have sanctioned the revival of traditional styles, the reintroduction of both classic and contemporary foreign works, and some experimentation with indigenous modern techniques. In intellectual matters, as well, there is greater freedom of academic inquiry, with fewer restrictions on the questions that can be researched and the views that can be expressed, even in areas with policy implications. In daily life, the party tolerates a wider degree of individual choice in matters of clothing, hobbies, personal appearance, and religious practice.

The results of this reform are apparent everywhere. As one casually strolls through any of China's major coastal cities, the eye is struck by the popularity of blue jeans and T-shirts among Chinese youth, and the ear is bombarded by the sounds of disco music coming from both public places and private homes. Discussions of political and academic issues in Chinese publications are more candid than in the past, with differences of opinion more openly expressed and acknowledged.

Less immediately obvious to the casual observer, but equally important to ordinary Chinese, has been the reduction of the power of basic-level economic enterprises over the daily affairs of the average peasant and worker. Before the reforms, factories provided their employees not only with a place of work but also with access to housing, medical treatment, day care, subsidized meals, recreation, and consumer goods that would not be readily available through other channels. In similar fashion, rural leaders exercised broad control over the economic fortunes of peasants, regulating their work assignments, their access to loans, their opportunities for outside employment, and often the size and location of their private plots. In each case, factory and commune officials had ample opportunity to distribute more goods and services to workers and peasants who stood in their good graces while giving less to those who had behaved less compliantly. But recent changes in economic policy are limiting both the control of factories over social services and the power of the collective over rural economic life. In so doing, the reforms are significantly reducing—although not completely eliminating—the ability of basic-level leaders to exercise arbitrary authority over their subordinates.[4]

The deregulation of these aspects of Chinese life has been accompanied by efforts to increase the predictability and regularity of those state controls that remain in effect. The degree to which the party and the state can exercise arbitrary power over society has been restricted by the creation of a legal framework specifying the substantive and procedural rights of Chinese citizens.[5] The state constitution of 1982, for example, contains more extensive and explicit statements of such rights as freedom of religious belief, the inviolability of the home, and privacy of correspondence than did any previous constitution. The criminal law and the code of criminal procedure provide guarantees against arbitrary arrest, arbitrary detention, and torture; more restrictive definitions of what constitute "counter-revolutionary acts"; and rights to a trial with a courtroom defense. Discriminatory political labels, assigned during the great political movements of the late Maoist period, have been removed from about 3 million "rightists" and "counter-revolutionaries," and pejorative class labels have been lifted from virtually all former landlords, rich peasants, and capitalists.[6]

Nonetheless, although the changes have been impressive, the reduction of the arbitrariness and scope of political controls remains limited. The revised legal system, for instance, still lacks key provisions considered crucial in much of Western law—notably, the presumption of innocence, guarantees against self-incrimination, and the acknowledgment that defense attorneys might actively attempt to discredit the case presented by the prosecution rather than merely plead for leniency in behalf of their clients. Furthermore, prominent political dissidents have occasionally been subjected to lengthy periods of detention without trial and to severe punishment for loosely defined offenses, thus suggesting that the state is willing to violate, in certain cases at least, even those rights and guarantees that have been granted to Chinese citizens by the recent legal reforms.[7]

In the same way, political intervention in social life has been narrowed but not eliminated. The freedoms granted since 1976 have often been qualified by countervailing constitutional duties and restrictions, such as the obligation to safeguard "the unity of the country" and "the security, honor, and interests of the motherland," and the prohibitions against actions that "infringe upon the interests of the state" or that "sabotage the socialist system." The party has reasserted its responsibility to create a "spiritual socialist civilization" in China, with "communist ideology at its core."[8] In the spring of 1979, Deng Xiaoping himself put forward four "basic principles" that are to be above dispute, thus making it impossible to question the leading role of the party, the basic structure of the state, the official commitment to Marxism, or the socialist orientation in development strategy.

In keeping with the residual rights of the state to preserve social order and the party's obligation to create a "socialist spiritual civilization," China has witnessed continuing campaigns against various kinds of deviant behavior since 1976. There have been harsh and intrusive birth control programs, periodic crackdowns against those who have overstepped the boundaries of politically permissible discourse, intense campaigns against crime and delinquency, and even, as during the movement against "spiritual pollution" in late 1983, restrictions on the ability of younger Chinese to wear more fashionable clothes and to go dancing in discos.

Nevertheless, each of these campaigns has been circumscribed. None has resembled the great mass movements against crime and political deviance in the 1950s, let alone the Cultural Revolution. Indeed, when the movement against "spiritual pollution" began to take on overtones similar to those associated with the Cultural Revolution, popular resentment, particularly among intellectuals, forced its cancellation. On balance, then, the degree to which today's Chinese enjoy the freedoms of inquiry, expression, and lifestyle, while not unlimited, far exceeds that during the final years of Mao's life and is arguably greater than at any time since 1949.

Expansion of Opportunities for Participation

The second broad route by which Chinese leaders have sought to overcome the political crisis of the mid-1970s has been to increase the channels for political participation, particularly for those groups whose involvement in politics is believed to contribute to economic modernization or whose support is deemed necessary to political stability.[9] The reform most worthy of note in this regard has been the development of a more active system of popular representation, with greater opportunities for electoral contestation at the grass-roots level and more extensive use of consultative mechanisms in the determination of policy at the national level.

In the past, the only government officials directly elected by their constituents were the delegates to the people's congresses at the lowest levels of Chinese society. All other legislative deputies were indirectly elected; all elections, whether direct or indirect, were noncompetitive; and all nominations to elective office were made by the party. Today, delegates to middle-level people's congresses, including those in rural counties and urban districts, are selected through direct election. What is more, the possibility remains that the use of direct elections will be extended to even higher levels of government in the future, although no timetable for such a development has been announced. More important, for the first time elections now involve competition for office, with one and a half to two times as many candidates as vacancies to be filled. Nominations, at least in theory, can come independently from groups of interested citizens, as well as from the official election committees controlled by the party.[10]

Such elections are significant, of course, only to the extent that they involve selection of officials to hold meaningful positions. And China's legislatures have, in fact, seen their roles expanded as compared with the Cultural Revolutionary period. This trend is particularly evident at the national level. The National People's Congress (NPC) has established a number of functional committees to discuss legislation; its Standing Committee meets frequently to consider matters of state; and the plenary sessions of the NPC have sometimes served as a forum for vigorous discussion of national policy and tough interrogation of state officials. State budgets and draft legislation have occasionally been modified slightly as a result of NPC discussions. And in refusing to adopt a resolution supporting the movement against "spiritual pollution" in December 1983, the Standing Committee of the NPC may have expressed for the first time a vote of no confidence toward a major party policy.

Other consultative mechanisms have also been given greater visibility in recent years. The post-Mao period has witnessed the revival of the smaller "democratic parties" and the Chinese People's Political Consultative Conference, both of which provide additional arenas in which intellectuals, scientists, and former capitalists can offer advice on government policy. Professional academic associations and research institutions are further channels through which scholars can express their views on national issues. Within economic enterprises, the reconstituted workers' congresses serve, to a limited degree, to represent the views of staff and workers to their supervisors; in some enterprises, managerial personnel are chosen through direct election by the workers.

Nonetheless, at the national level, and to an even greater degree in the localities, people's congresses remain essentially consultative and advisory bodies. They have not yet become independent assemblies that can veto, initiate, or meaningfully alter legislation, or that can impose accountability on state officials. Motions introduced at legislative sessions are not voted upon collectively; rather, they serve as petitions or inquiries that administrative bodies must eventually respond to but need not necessarily adopt. Congresses meet infrequently in short sessions; delegates are not full-time representatives and have no staff. A recent summary of the situation at the urban district level probably applies to higher legislative bodies as well: "Deputies may be able to raise issues where local leaders are guilty of malfeasance or otherwise out of step with policies laid down by higher levels, or to make suggestions regarding specific problems encountered by their constituents. However, they seem unable to build independent power bases, to initiate general changes in policy, or [to] legislate reform."[11]

Moreover, there have been several cases in which local officials have not faithfully implemented the spirit of the new electoral system. Local cadres have refused to nominate more than one candidate for each office, have overruled election returns that did not produce the desired results, and have harassed those few candidates, particularly in university constituencies, who chose to raise fundamental questions about the direction of society and the nature of the political structure.[12]

Finally, restrictions remain on the forms that participation may take. Although candidates for public office are permitted to express their preferences on political issues, they are prohibited by regulation from doing so in ways that would appeal to regional or class interests. The rights to hold "revolutionary great debates" and to write wall posters, which were legacies of the Cultural Revolution, were removed from the constitution by amendment in 1980 on the grounds that such activities might libel innocent officials or promote political disunity. The right to strike was quietly dropped from the new constitution adopted in 1982, probably with an eye to contemporary developments in Poland. Unsanctioned organizations, including professional associations and trade unions, have been required to disband; in addition, unlicensed periodicals, such as the dissident journals that flourished during the "Peking Spring" of 1979, when the democratic movement reached its peak, have been forced to suspend publication. On the other hand, the state constitution does still permit street demonstrations, and they occasionally occur, particularly on college campuses.

Thus, although political participation has expanded since 1976, the party and state retain the power to restrict it to regularized consultative mechanisms and to deny it to unsanctioned publications and associations. Above all, the right to form autonomous political organizations, independent of party control, does not yet exist in post-Mao China.

Revitalization of Administrative Institutions

After 1976, China faced two serious administrative problems as its new leaders redirected national attention from the task of continuous revolution to that of sustained modernization. The first was the relative inability of the country's overaged and underskilled bureaucratic institutions to manage an increasingly complex economy. The solution to this first problem has been (1) to restaff the party and state bureaucracies so as to develop a corps of cadres that is younger, better educated, more professional, and more committed to reform, and then (2) to revamp the nation's civil service policies so as to institutionalize these initial achievements.[13] Second, as one further legacy of the totalitarianism of the late-Mao period, the party unduly monopolized all matters of public administration. Consequently, the reform program in post-Mao China has also witnessed efforts to loosen the control of the party over the government and enterprise management.[14]

The restaffing of the party and state bureaucracies—a process that began at the central level in 1982 and was extended to the basic levels in 1984—has involved a degree of personnel turnover reminiscent of the sweeping purges of the Cultural Revolution. By June 1983, fully thirty-three of thirty-seven cabinet members, ten of twenty-nine provincial first party secretaries, and twenty-six of twenty-nine heads of provincial government had been removed from office. A second round of personnel rotations, this time involving the armed forces as well as the civilian bureaucracy, began in mid-1985. At lower echelons, 44 percent of the leading officials at the provincial levels, and nearly 50 percent of those at the prefectural levels, have been newly appointed since the reorganization began.[15]

The effect of these turnovers on the age and level of education of China's administrators has been impressive. At the central level, the average age of ministers and vice-ministers was reduced from 64 to 58, of directors and deputy directors of party departments from 64 to 60, and of directors and deputy directors of state bureaus from 59 to 54. At the provincial level the average age of officials is now around 55, and in prefectures and municipalities it has dropped to 50. The proportion of officials with a college education ranges from 45 percent at lower levels to 50 percent in Peking, and the goal is to ensure, through a combination of replacement and retraining, that all officials in the state and party bureaucracy will have the level of a senior middle-school education within five years.[16]

To perpetuate these benefits, Chinese organizational policy has been changed to provide, for the first time, regular procedures for recruitment, rotation, promotion, and retirement in the party and state bureaucracies.[17] Recruitment standards are stricter, with priority now placed on recruiting university graduates for the civil service. Cadres are subject to regular appraisals of their performance, reportedly on the basis of a clear definition of the responsibilities of their position, and the appraisals become the basis for promotion and reward. The state constitution specifies a two-term limit, totaling ten years, for the president, prime minister, vice-premiers, and ministers; in addition, party regulations provide that all party members who serve in official positions in either the party or the state, except for certain ill-defined "specialists," are to be rotated every five to ten years.

Finally, for the first time in the history of the People's Republic, a retirement age has been set for state and party officials: 65 for principal leaders at the national and provincial levels, 60 for their deputies and for principal leaders at the prefectural level, and, for all other officials, 60 for men and 55 for women. To ease the transition, superannuated senior cadres have been retired at full or even increased pay, guaranteed continued access to official documents, provided prestigious appointments as consultants or advisers, allowed to keep their drivers and secretaries, and given preferential treatment in the allocation of housing. By April 1985, 900,000 older cadres had been retired, with another 1 million expected to hand over their duties to younger officials by the end of 1986.[18]

If revitalizing and rationalizing the composition of the party and state bureaucracies constitutes one aspect of institutional restructuring, a second and potentially more important development has been the reduction of the role of the party in day-to-day administration. That role had increased in China rather steadily throughout the Maoist period, with the exception of a brief interlude during the turmoil at the height of the Cultural Revolution. The growing power of the party over other organizations reflected the Maoist desire to concentrate power in the hands of ideologically committed generalists and to tighten party control over all other institutions. Indeed, by the late 1960s, the government was being described as a duplicative and unnecessary bureaucracy; by the early 1970s, it had been explicitly relegated to the position of serving as the administrative arm of the Communist party.

By the end of the decade, however, the costs of such an arrangement had become increasingly apparent, particularly as priorities began to shift from revolution to modernization. Chinese leaders acknowledged that the merger of "party leadership" with "administrative and vocational work" was highly inefficient, inasmuch as a party of 40 million members, and only 9 million administrative officials, could not possibly make all decisions for a country of 1 billion people. Moreover, the party's monopoly of power, at the expense of more broadly representative organizations, was alienating it from much of society. Chinese leaders also warned that the party risked neglecting its fundamental responsibilities—such as monitoring the performance of the state bureaucracy and economic enterprises, and educating society in socialist values and Marxist doctrine—if it remained preoccupied with administrative detail.

But there is a second set of reasons why the role of the party had to be redefined—one its leaders have not yet publicly acknowledged. As Valerie Bunce pointed out in a recent study of Eastern Europe, the Communist party occupies both a monopolistic and a monopsonistic position in a Soviet-style political system.[19] In other words, it is the sole producer of political decisions and the sole consumer of political demands. As opportunities for political participation increase (an inevitable consequence of socioeconomic modernization), the demands placed on the party grow apace. In order to insulate itself from those demands and to preserve a greater degree of organizational autonomy, the party grants to other institutions both the power to make secondary decisions and the responsibility to cope with growing political pressures from society at large. In so doing, the party may be giving up its monopoly over administrative matters, but it will thereby maintain its ability to deal effectively with overall policy questions.

As a result of these considerations, other Chinese organizations, particularly the state bureaucracy, are being granted greater autonomy from the party in their day-to-day operations. For the most part, officials in the party apparatus no longer hold concurrent positions as state officials. Provincial governors, factory managers, directors of research institutes, and university presidents are all being given increasing powers to appoint their own subordinates and to make administrative decisions, without direct intervention by the relevant party committees.

Nonetheless, the party retains several basic powers that deserve mention. It still sets national policy guidelines, although most must now be established in legal form by the legislative organs and implemented by the government bureaucracy rather than by the party itself. Thus, all the recent economic reform measures—from the agricultural reform of January 1984 to the urban economic reform of October 1984 to the reform of science and technology in March 1985—have been issued first as party documents, drafted by the Party Secretariat, rather than as government regulations. Despite recommendations to the contrary, the party retains control over appointments to the state bureaucracy, as well as over elections to people's congresses. Party members serving as state officials—or as leaders in any "people's organization, economic or cultural institution or other non-Party unit"—are organized into party fractions, or cells, whose job it is "to see to it that the party's principles and policies are implemented."[20] All these powers suggest that the party's authority over political matters remains broad, even though the extent of its direct control is less deep than before.

Normalization of Elite Politics

The fractiousness of Chinese politics in 1976—characterized by bitter struggles among competing leaders, continual maneuvering for advantageous positions, and factional strategies to preserve or extend bases of political power—posed a potential threat to the implementation of reform and the stability of the system after the death of Deng Xiaoping. Accordingly, a high priority has been placed on measures to recreate a working consensus among the elite and to restore stability to elite-level politics.[21]

Attempts to promote leadership unity have involved, first, a reshuffling of the party, state, and military organizations so as to increase support for reform. At the central level, the results have been most striking in the Party Secretariat, the Central Committee, and the State Council; somewhat less pronounced in the Politburo; and only preliminary in the military establishment. Deng Xiaoping has been quite successful in securing the removal, demotion, or neutralization of those associated with the Cultural Revolution or Hua Guofeng, but less successful in reducing the power of those who would prefer a more cautious approach to reform than the sweeping changes envisioned by Deng, Hu Yaobang, and Zhao Ziyang.

Second, a significant change has occurred in the party's recruitment policies. During the decade of the Cultural Revolution, emphasis was placed on drawing into party membership the underprivileged of society, particularly poor and lower-middle peasants and urban workers. Of the 40 million members of the party today, about 18 million, or 45 percent, were recruited under those criteria. Recruitment standards have recently been redefined in favor of those who are presumed to be the beneficiaries, and thus the supporters, of reform—particularly urban intellectuals and the most prosperous peasants. Over time, this reform is designed to supplement unity among the elite with greater unity within the vanguard party organization.

In order to restore normalcy to inner-party politics, Chinese leaders have attempted to revive the traditional norms of Chinese Communist political life—rules that were codified in Yan'an after the ruthless internal struggles of the 1920s and 1930s, which were reasserted in the early 1950s and then shattered by Mao Zedong during the last two decades of his leadership. Some of these norms concern the management of political conflict within the party. They involve an implicit bargain within the party elite under which the protection of minority rights is exchanged for loyalty to majority rule. According to these arrangements, party members agree to follow party discipline, to implement even those party decisions with which they disagree, and to advocate their preferred policies through orderly and peaceful procedures. In return, they are guaranteed that they will be governed by a system of collective leadership, that the power of individual leaders will be limited, that those whose interests are involved will be consulted in the determination of policy, and that the rights of those who take minority positions will be safeguarded. The resuscitation of these traditional norms has been supported by leaders across a wide spectrum of political opinion. Indeed, it was one of the first tasks undertaken by Hua Guofeng during his brief interregnum after the death of Mao.

Other norms concern the balance between military and civilian leadership in China. Mao's precept that "the Party should control the gun" was violated during the Cultural Revolution, when, as a means of restoring political order, the military was allowed to dominate most provincial governments and to occupy about 45 percent of the seats on the Central Committee. Personnel changes after the purge of Lin Biao reduced the military's role somewhat, but the armed forces still entered the post-Mao period with a degree of representation in the party unprecedented since the earliest years of the People's Republic.

Since the late 1970s, however, China has seen the recivilianization of political life. Military officers have been removed from virtually all provincial-level party and government positions, and from most positions on the State Council. Although the People's Liberation Army (PLA) retains substantial power on the Politburo, holding eight seats out of twenty-seven, its representation on the Central Committee was reduced to 19 percent at the Twelfth Party Congress in 1982, roughly the same ratio that prevailed during the mid-1950s. The army remains an important actor in Chinese politics, but it has increasingly become one interest group among many, without the power to impose its wishes upon the civilian establishment.

In addition to all these measures to restore unity and normalcy, the party launched a three-year rectification campaign that is still working its way down the party hierarchy from the center to the grass-roots level. Although a small number of party members (probably around 0.1 percent) will be expelled or disciplined, and although some party branches will be reorganized, the emphasis thus far has been on political education, particularly on the desirability of the reform program, and on the need to eliminate the factional legacy of the Cultural Revolution years.

Once again, however, it is important that we not overstate the achievements won by China's reformers. The restoration of party unity will require a lengthy process, particularly given the radical character of Deng Xiaoping's program of economic reform and the fact that so large a proportion of the party was recruited during the Cultural Revolution. Nor should the degree of party institutionalization be exaggerated. While touting the virtues of organizational regularization, party leaders still implement many of their programs—including the reeducation and restaffing of the party itself—through the medium of political campaigns. And although Deng has sought to deny others in the party the right to engage in factional conflict, he himself waged just such a struggle against his hapless predecessor, Hua Guofeng, and has sanctioned the attempts of his heir apparent, Hu Yaobang, to build a personal base of power within the party apparatus. In short, the process of political institutionalization remains incomplete, and its results remain untested.

Redefinition of the Basis of Authority

A final aspect of political reform involves a redefinition of the basis of authority in Chinese political life—a change in the grounds on which the party seeks to legitimate its rule. In general terms, the past eight years have seen a decline in the relative importance of charisma and ideology, as well as a rise of more secular and pragmatic forms of political authority. Nonetheless, this transformation has not gone so far as to allow us to conclude that China has repudiated Marxism, or that it has completely eliminated the exercise of personalistic leadership.

The decline in charismatic authority in China began with the Third Plenum of December 1978, which condemned the personality cult surrounding Mao Zedong, implicitly criticized the attempts to inflate the personal prestige of Hua Guofeng, and announced a new period of collective leadership. Mao's errors were acknowledged in increasingly frank and direct terms, and his political and ideological accomplishments were redefined as the result of collective party leadership rather than of personal genius. Symbolic of the decharismatization of the late chairman was the transformation of the Mao Zedong Memorial Hall, in the heart of Peking's Tiananmen Square, into a memorial to the entire Long March generation of party leaders—instead of a monument to Mao himself. Further measures have included the removal of Mao's portraits from most public spaces and the more sparing use of his quotations in Chinese publications.

Changes have also occurred in the party's attitude toward ideology. The content of official doctrine has been almost completely transformed. The party has repudiated all the major tenets of late Maoism: that class struggle remains the principal contradiction in socialist society, that bourgeois ideas are likely to appear in their most dangerous form within the party itself, that combating bourgeois ideas requires a continuous revolutionary struggle by the proletariat, and that campaigns of mass criticism against "party people in authority taking the capitalist road" are the most suitable forms for undertaking such a struggle. Others, such as Mao's "theory of the three worlds," have been quietly deemphasized. Concepts such as humanism and alienation, associated with early Marxism but officially proscribed for many years, are now being rediscovered. A more critical attitude is being taken in some intellectual circles toward Lenin's theories of imperialism and the vanguard party.

Second, the role of ideology has been reduced. Chinese leaders now acknowledge that a wide range of intellectual, scientific, and technical questions can be discussed without reference to ideological principles. The result is that a larger number of policy matters can be addressed on their own merits, relatively unconstrained by doctrinal considerations. Moreover, even in those areas in which it is deemed to be relevant, ideology is no longer regarded as a dogma that provides specific and infallible solutions to immediate political issues; instead, it is treated as a bundle of methods for analyzing policy problems and as a set of broad goals for the future.[22]

None of this, however, should be interpreted either as the complete elimination of personalistic authority or as the repudiation of ideology. Although China today is no longer a system organized exclusively around the rule of a single charismatic leader, central authority in China, as in other Asian countries, remains focused to a large degree upon the personal prestige of a paramount leader, namely Deng Xiaoping. Despite the fact that he holds few formal positions in the party or state apparatus, the Chinese themselves openly acknowledge that Deng still makes or approves all major policy decisions. Moreover, he enjoys quasi-charismatic standing among those Chinese who approve of his reforms, and his *Selected Works* are standard reading assignments in all political education programs, much as Mao's were before him.

Similarly, Marxism is still defined as the official orthodoxy of the Communist state, and considerable effort is still spent in its exegesis. The appeal of Marxism to the party, and to many intellectuals, stems from both political and cultural considerations. The leadership of the Communist party still rests to a large degree on the notion that it embodies a scientifically correct body of doctrine, which justifies its rule. If the party were actually to repudiate Marxism, it would not only remove an important underpinning of its own legitimacy but might well usher in a period of political uncertainty and instability, which the overwhelming majority of Chinese seek to avoid.

Further, many Chinese appear convinced that today, as much as in imperial times, governing as vast a country as China requires the unifying force of an official ideology as well as the integrative power of national political institutions. As one provincial official put it in late 1983, "A ruling party and state cannot do without its own guiding ideology, and the condition of its guiding ideology is related to the prosperity or decline of the state."[23] In the eyes of most Chinese intellectuals, the principal ideological alternatives in the contemporary world are socialism and capitalism. To adopt capitalism would not only require a repudiation of Marxism, with all the difficulties already mentioned; it would also sanction precisely the forces of individualism, competition, and pluralism that are believed to threaten the unity of the country. Like Confucianism before it, Marxism emphasizes collectivism, cooperation, and national unity—values that can better serve to protect China against the centrifugal influences originating at the grass-roots level.

Although Marxism will not likely be repudiated, nor will personal authority completely disappear, it is true that the relative importance of both ideology and charisma in contemporary China has been markedly reduced. Rising in their place is a mixture of more secular and pragmatic elements. The classic Weberian alternative—rational-legal authority—does play a part, as suggested by the greater utilization of intellectuals and experts and by the attempts to ground political life in constitutions, laws, and statutory procedures. But more important are two additional forms of authority—nationalism and modernization—which Weber did not foresee explicitly but which have been important sources of legitimacy for most developing states in the latter half of this century. The party increasingly rests its authority on the claims that it embodies the political aspirations of a billion Chinese and is implementing policies that will achieve the long-standing ideal of a "strong state and a rich people." Thus Marxism is being redefined as a flexible program of economic development rather than as a rigid blueprint for social revolution, and the Chinese people are being reassured that the socialism sought by their leaders will be one with "Chinese characteristics," rather than one that is copied from the Soviet or Eastern European experience.

How strong a basis of authority is now provided by this blend of ideology and nationalism, personalism and legality, and rationality and economic performance? The legitimacy of the regime is certainly greater now than it was in 1976, and it is possible to argue that the "crisis of confidence" that existed at the time of Mao's death has been largely overcome. And yet, in some respects, the system still rests on a fragile foundation. Official ideology has become increasingly vague, its exegeses are growing more vapid, and it appears to meet with widespread disinterest outside certain intellectual circles. Appeals to rational and legal authority are limited by the fact that the party is fully bound by neither expertise nor law. It still denies intellectuals the right freely to investigate certain fundamental political issues and, as we shall see, views legality more as an instrument of its rule than as a constraint upon it. The prestige of Deng Xiaoping and the performance of the economy serve well for the moment, but they may not be adequate sources of legitimacy for the longer term—for one will certainly die and the other may well falter. That leaves nationalism, which has been a powerful force in modern Chinese history but is rarely the property solely of the regime in power. The claim to embody the aspirations of the Chinese people is one that can be made by any indigenous political force, be it government or opposition.

Conclusion

How, then, can one evaluate the political evolution of China in the post-Mao era? Undeniably, much has been accomplished. Authority has become more secular, the political process more regular, and political institutions more responsive. There is more freedom for individual Chinese—both freedom from the arbitrary power of the state and freedom to participate in public affairs. A good start has been made in modernizing the Chinese bureaucracy. Although the institutions of totalitarianism have not been completely dismantled, they have been deactivated sufficiently that China no longer warrants the label of a totalitarian system.

And yet there are also limits on the degree to which the Chinese political system has been reformed. Some of these limits reflect what has been attempted but not yet achieved. Despite the achievements in restoring stability to political life, for example, it is not yet certain that the crisis created by the Cultural Revolution has been completely resolved. It remains to be seen how smoothly China's post-Mao political system will weather the death of Deng Xiaoping, on whose personal prestige so much still rests, and whose reform measures remain so controversial. Nor is it clear whether the regime has adequate reserves of legitimacy to avoid dissent and disorder if economic growth rates slow, or if reforms produce greater levels of inequality, inflation, unemployment, or corruption. Moreover, given the shift in the relative power of state and society in recent years, popular discontent could take on increasingly disruptive forms in post-Deng China, as evidenced by recent protests and sit-ins in the heart of Peking and other major cities.

But not all the shortcomings in China's contemporary political system stem from what has been tried but not achieved. Other limits on the political development of post-Mao China reflect those reforms that have not even been sought by Deng Xiaoping and his colleagues.

Three distinctions may help us understand the boundaries that the reformers have placed on their own political and organizational program. First, while China is becoming more consultative, it has not yet become truly pluralistic. Political organizations do not enjoy independence from party control. The right to contest for political office is still limited, for the most part, to candidates nominated or approved by the party. Restrictions remain on the form, content, and extent of political participation. In short, although public involvement in political life has increased since 1976, it is still licensed by the party rather than completely autonomous.[24]

Second, although China is increasingly ruled *by* law, it is not yet an example of the rule *of* law.[25] Rule by law reflects a situation in which the state chooses to employ administrative regulations and criminal codes to enforce its policies in a predictable way. The rule of law, in contrast, implies that citizens have procedural and substantive rights, guaranteed by the constitution, which the state cannot violate at will. Although rule by law characterizes China more today than at any other time in the history of the People's Republic, it is not yet clear that the party accepts the existence of enduring legal procedures that unconditionally protect citizens against its control.

Third, in a stimulating discussion of the scope of political control over contemporary Chinese society, Tang Tsou has distinguished between "spheres of immunity" and "spheres of indifference."[26] The former are those areas of social life in which the state acknowledges in a binding and enduring manner that it has no right to interfere; the latter, in contrast, are those areas in which the state simply chooses not to involve itself for the time being, without renouncing the right to intervene in the future. Clearly, the sphere of indifference has greatly widened in post-Mao China. But, in keeping with long-standing Chinese views on the role of the state in promoting moral civilization, that indifference has not yet been translated into a firm sphere of immunity.

The common denominator linking these three aspects of contemporary political life in China is that Chinese leaders still seem to regard democracy, legality, and freedom as means to other goals rather than as ends in themselves. Freedom is required to encourage scientific creativity and economic initiative; legality is necessary to increase predictability and maintain popular support; and democratization is essential to resolve the crisis of confidence that separated large sectors of the Chinese people from their government. Yet all of these reforms have been implemented conditionally, subject to the premise that these new rights will not be used in ways that violate the remaining limits on what is politically permissible.

Thus, in assessing political development in post-Mao China, we must not confuse the *direction* of change with the actual *outcomes* of reform. By making elections more competitive, by increasing the role of representative assemblies, and by reducing the extent of party control over state and society, China has indeed become much more pluralistic than it was in the late Mao period. But these reforms do not mean that China has yet become, in absolute terms, a pluralistic system, characterized by the possibility for independent political organization and contestation for public office.[27] Similarly, although many of the reforms have been motivated by the need to effect a reconciliation between a seriously decayed state and an increasingly alienated society, the measures taken thus far have not transformed China into what David Apter has termed a "reconciliation system," characterized by full, effective, and autonomous popular participation in public deci-sionmaking.[28]

Rather, China in the early post-Mao period has become what might best be described as a "consultative authoritarian" regime, a significant departure from the totalitarianism of the recent past but not yet a fully democratic, or even a quasi-pluralistic, political system.[29] It is increasingly consultative in its recognition of the need to obtain information, advice, and support from key sectors of the population, but still authoritarian in its desire to suppress dissent and maintain ultimate political power in the hands of the party. Moreover, by denying the possibility of an organized opposition, even in limited form, today's China stands in contrast to other East Asian political regimes, such as South Korea and Taiwan, in which opposition forces are either tacitly or formally allowed to exist in what remain relatively authoritarian systems.

In this way, Chinese politics today still retains many of the char-acteristics of Soviet politics since the dismissal of Nikita Khrushchev. At first glance, this failure to depart decisively from the post-Stalinist model of politics may seem somewhat surprising. The economic challenge facing China in the mid-1970s was, as we have seen, much less acute than the political crisis. And yet, Chinese leaders acted more boldly in the economic realm than in the political sphere. They were prepared to make an explicit break from the Soviet model of economic planning and management, and from Soviet patterns of foreign economic policy. But they have not chosen to make a comparably clear departure from Soviet principles of political organization. This relative caution reflects their understanding that substantial economic liberalization can be undertaken without challenging the rule of the party, but also that a similar degree of political reform would probably have destabilizing consequences.

To be sure, many Chinese point to differences between their political system and that of the Soviet Union. It is true that Moscow has not yet adopted competitive elections, instituted fixed terms of office for government and party officials, or experimented with a reduction in the scale of party rule to the same degree as China has done. It may also be the case, as some Chinese claim, that the arbitrary personal power of individual leaders in China, particularly at lower levels of society, is now less than that in the Soviet Union. Such dissimilarities do make Chinese politics somewhat more liberal than Soviet politics. Still, these are differences of degree, not of kind. They are not yet sufficient to allow the conclusion that the Chinese political system is fundamentally different from that of the post-Stalinist Soviet Union.

For the future, the intriguing question is whether the processes of economic modernization and reform now under way will lead to a more thoroughgoing liberalization of Chinese politics, and to its further transformation into, perhaps, a quasi-pluralistic authoritarianism. The demands for such political reform do exist, particularly among some younger urban intellectuals, and may well increase along with levels of education and exposure to Western ideas. But the resistance to those demands within the party is still strong, and will probably remain so. Moreover, most Chinese appear to believe that further liberalization would not be congruent with China's slowly changing political culture, nor with the level of popular education outside the country's major cities.

For the rest of the century, therefore, what is most likely is not any fundamental reordering of the current political system but, rather, its development and elaboration. China may see the expansion of the powers of legislative bodies, the extension of direct elections to higher levels of administration, a continued increase in the average education of government officials, greater expression of opinions by bureaucratic agencies, and further state consultation with officially sanctioned mass organizations. It may also see the rise of urban-based protest, either organized or spontaneous. But it is unlikely that the hallmarks of genuine pluralism—autonomous political organizations and independent contestation for political power—will emerge.

Notes

1. My understanding of the basic characteristics of Stalinism is drawn largely from Seweryn Bialer, *Stalin's Successors: Leadership, Stability, and Change in the Soviet Union* (Cambridge, England: Cambridge University Press, 1980), chs. 1–3; and Stephen Cohen, "Bolshevism and Stalinism," in Robert C. Tucker (ed.), *Stalinism: Essays in Historical Interpretation* (New York: Norton,

1977), pp. 3–29. For a brief comparison of Stalinism and Maoism, see Thomas P. Bernstein, "How Stalinist Was Mao's China?" *Problems of Communism* 34, no. 2 (March-April 1985), pp. 118–125.

2. Samuel P. Huntington, *Political Order in Changing Societies* (New Haven, Conn.: Yale University Press, 1968), ch. 1.

3. The most comprehensive discussions of political reform by Chinese leaders occurred in the latter part of 1980. The stimulus was a major speech by Deng Xiaoping to an enlarged meeting of the Politburo on August 18, entitled "On the Reform of the System of Party and State Leadership." A revised version of that speech appears in *Selected Works of Deng Xiaoping (1975–1982)* (Peking: Foreign Languages Press, 1984), pp. 302–325. Two important exegeses of Deng's speech by leading party intellectuals are Feng Wenbin's "On the Question of Socialist Democracy," *Renmin Ribao,* November 24 and 25, 1980, reprinted in *Foreign Broadcast Information Service, Daily Report: People's Republic of China* (hereafter *FBIS-CHI*), November 26, 1980, pp. L23–L30, and December 2, 1980, pp. L9–L15; and Liao Gailong's "Advance Along the Road of Chinese-Style Socialist Construction Which Has Been Selected by the Party," *Ch'i-shih nien-tai* (Hong Kong), no. 134 (March 1, 1981), in *FBIS-CHI*, March 16, 1981, pp. U1–U19.

4. On the dependency of workers and peasants on basic-level leaders, see Andrew G. Walder, "Organized Dependency and Cultures of Authority in Chinese Industry," *Journal of Asian Studies* 43, no. 1 (November 1983), pp. 51–76; and Jean C. Oi, "Communism and Clientelism: Rural Politics in China," *World Politics* 37, no. 2 (January 1985), pp. 238–266.

5. On the post-Mao legal order, see Richard Baum, "China's Post-Mao Legal Reforms in Historical and Comparative Perspective," paper presented to conference, "To Reform the Chinese Political Order," Harwichport, Mass., June 1984; Frances Hoar Foster, "Codification in Post-Mao China," *American Journal of Comparative Law* 30, no. 3 (Summer 1982), pp. 395–428; Shao-chuan Leng, "Criminal Justice in Post-Mao China," *China Quarterly*, no. 87 (September 1981), pp. 440–469; and Byron Weng, "Some Key Aspects of the 1982 Draft Constitution of the People's Republic of China," *China Quarterly*, no. 91 (September 1982), pp. 492–506.

6. On the rehabilitation of such erstwhile "pariah groups," see Hong Yung Lee, "Changing Patterns of Political Participation in China: A Historical Perspective," paper presented to workshop, "Studies in Policy Implementation in the Post-Mao Era," Columbus, Ohio, June 1983.

7. For a discussion of the limits on legalization, especially where dissent is at issue, see Amnesty International, *China: Violations of Human Rights* (London: Amnesty International Publications, 1984).

8. Hu Yaobang, "Create a New Situation in All Fields of Socialist Modernization," September 1, 1982, in *The Twelfth National Congress of the CPC* (Peking: Foreign Languages Press, 1982), p. 38.

9. For another treatment of the expansion of political participation in post-Mao China, see Brantly Womack, "Modernization and Democratic Reform in China," *Journal of Asian Studies* 43, no. 3 (May 1984), pp. 417–440.

10. On elections, see Andrew J. Nathan, *Chinese Democracy* (New York: Alfred A. Knopf, 1985), ch. 10; and Brantly Womack, "The 1980 County-Level Elections in China: Experiment in Democratic Modernization," *Asian Survey* 22, no. 3 (March 1982), pp. 261–277.

11. Barrett L. McCormick, "Reforming the People's Congress System: A Case Study of the Implementation of 'Strengthening Socialist Law and Socialist Democracy' in Post-Mao China," paper presented to workshop, "Studies in Policy Implementation in the Post-Mao Era," Columbus, Ohio, June 1983.

12. Nathan, *Chinese Democracy*, ch. 10.

13. On the revitalization of the administrative organizations, see Maria Chan Morgan, "Controlling the Bureaucracy in Post-Mao China," *Asian Survey* 21, no. 12 (December 1981), pp. 1223–1236; Hong Yung Lee, "China's 12th Central Committee: Rehabilitated Cadres and Technocrats," *Asian Survey* 23, no. 6 (June 1983), pp. 673–691; John P. Burns, "Reforming China's Bureaucracy, 1979–82," *Asian Survey* 23, no. 6 (June 1983), pp. 692–722; and Victor C. Falkenheim, "Institutionalization and Reform in China's Party-State Structure," in *Mainland China's Modernization: Its Prospects and Problems*, proceedings of the Tenth Sino-American Conference on Mainland China (Taipei and Berkeley: Institute of International Studies and Institute of East Asian Studies, University of California at Berkeley, 1981), pp. 50–61.

14. For a further discussion of the changing role of the party in post-Mao China, see Harry Harding, "The Reform of the Chinese Communist Party," paper presented to conference, "To Reform the Chinese Political Order," Harwichport, Mass., June 1984.

15. Kazuko Mori, "First Session of 6th NPC—Groundwork for Post-Deng Era," *JETRO China Newsletter* (Tokyo), no. 46 (June 1983), pp. 8–14; Christopher M. Clarke, "China's Reform Program," *Current History* 83, no. 494 (September 1984), pp. 254–256, 273; and *Liaowang*, no. 21 (May 21, 1984), in *FBIS-CHI*, June 18, 1984, pp. K7–K10.

16. Xinhua [New China News Agency], January 5, 1984, in *FBIS-CHI*, January 5, 1984, p. K8; Xinhua, January 22, 1984, in *FBIS-CHI*, January 23, 1984, pp. K1–K2; and Xinhua, January 23, 1984, in *FBIS-CHI*, January 25, 1984, pp. K21–K24.

17. On the institutionalization of the cadre system, see Melanie Manion (ed.), "Cadre Recruitment and Management in the People's Republic of China," *Chinese Law and Government* 17, no. 3 (Fall 1984), pp. 1–128. This issue includes a translation of a booklet prepared by the Organization Bureau, Research Office, Organization Department, Central Committee of the Chinese Communist Party, entitled *Dang de zuzhi gongzuo wenda* [Questions and Answers on Party Organization Work] (Peking: Remin Chubanshe, 1983).

18. *Hsin Wan Pao* (Hong Kong), April 9, 1985, in *FBIS-CHI*, April 9, 1985, pp. W1–W2.

19. Valerie Bunce, "The Empire Strikes Back: The Evolution of the Eastern Bloc from a Soviet Asset to a Soviet Liability," *International Organization* 39, no. 1 (Winter 1985), pp. 1–46, at p. 29.

20. "Constitution of the Communist Party of China," September 1982, in *Twelfth National Congress*, p. 129.

21. This section draws on my chapter, "Political Stability and Succession," in U.S. Congress, Joint Economic Committee, *The Chinese Economy in the Eighties,* forthcoming.

22. On the transformation of ideology in post-Mao China, see Helmut Martin, *Cult and Canon: The Origins and Development of State Maoism* (Armonk, N.Y.: M. E. Sharpe, 1982); and Tang Tsou, "The Historic Change in Direction and Continuity with the Past," *China Quarterly,* no. 98 (June 1984), pp. 320–347.

23. Radio Nanning, December 25, 1983, in *FBIS-CHI,* December 28, 1983, pp. P3–P5.

24. The concept of licensed participation is drawn from David G. Strand, "Reform of Political Participation," paper presented to conference, "To Reform the Chinese Political Order," Harwichport, Massachusetts, June 1984.

25. This distinction is developed in Baum, "China's Post-Mao Legal Reforms."

26. Tang Tsou, "Back from the Brink of Revolutionary-'Feudal' Totalitarianism," in Victor Nee and David Mozingo (eds.), *State and Society in Contemporary China* (Ithaca, N.Y.: Cornell University Press, 1983), pp. 53–88.

27. The defining characteristics of pluralism are those suggested by Cyril E. Black and John P. Burke, "Organizational Participation and Public Policy," *World Politics* 35, no. 3 (April 1983), pp. 393–425.

28. David Apter, *The Politics of Modernization* (Chicago: University of Chicago Press, 1965).

29. I have drawn the term *consultative authoritarianism* from H. Gordon Skilling, "Group Conflict and Political Change," in Chalmers Johnson (ed.), *Change in Communist Systems* (Stanford, Calif.: Stanford University Press, 1970), pp. 215–234.

2
The Prospects for China's Economic Reforms

Dwight H. Perkins

After seven years of uninterrupted efforts at economic reform, there is little doubt that China has departed in major ways from the system it adopted from the Soviet Union in the 1950s. Will these reform efforts continue into the future, or, like the Cultural Revolution before them, will they lead to reversal? For that matter, will the changes result in abandonment of a Soviet-style economy, or will the reforms go only part of the way and result in an economy that preserves key features of the Soviet system, modified by the post-1976 reforms? No one in or outside China has a definitive answer to these questions, but a review of the events of the past decade does provide a basis for informed speculation.

The Economic Legacy of the Cultural Revolution

The period of the Cultural Revolution (1966–1976) is widely perceived as one of uninterrupted disaster for Chinese society as a whole, including the economy. At the political and personal levels this image is accurate enough. Lives were torn apart; many died, often by their own hands; and national politics was wracked by dissension and attempted coups connected with the question of who would succeed Mao Zedong as leader of China.

But China's economy during this decade of political turmoil did not fare all that badly. The political battles involving urban workers and students during the early years of the Cultural Revolution did disrupt industrial production, but full recovery and renewed growth were achieved in most sectors by 1969 and in the remaining sectors by 1970 (see Table 2.1). In fact, during the entire eleven years from the beginning of 1966 through the end of 1976, the gross value of industrial output grew at an annual average rate of 9.5 percent—

Table 2.1
Output Indexes in the Cultural Revolution

	1965	1966	1967	1968	1969	1970	1975
Gross value of industrial output	83	100	86	82	110	144	222
-Electric power	82	100	94	87	114	140	237
-Steel	80	100	67	59	87	116	156
-Petroleum	78	100	95	110	149	211	530
-Cloth	86	100	90	88	112	125	129
-Bicycles	90	100	86	97	142	180	304
Gross value of agricultural output	92	100	102	99	100	112	136
-Grain	91	100	102	98	99	112	133

Source: State Statistical Bureau, Statistical Yearbook of China, 1983
(Hong Kong: Economic Information and Agency, 1983).

down from the 12.3 percent average of 1952 to 1965, but still quite a high rate in international comparative terms.[1]

Agricultural production suffered even less from the political chaos. Over the eleven-year period 1966–1976, grain output and the gross value of agricultural output declined in only three years (1968, 1969, and 1972), and those declines were due at least partly to weather. The annual average growth rate of the grain sector over the same period was 3.6 percent, considerably higher than the 1.3 percent annual average rate between 1952 and 1965. The figures for the earlier period are distorted by the tremendously disruptive impact of the Great Leap Forward (1958–1960), but the basic point remains. China's economy was not submerged in a deep and prolonged recession during the Cultural Revolution. It was growing at an unremarkable but nevertheless quite respectable rate.

What, then, triggered the post-1976 reform effort? The answer, in part, is that China's "good" economic performance from 1966 through 1976 was deceptive. There were at least two reasons for believing that this performance could not be sustained if the policies of the Cultural Revolution period were not modified. First, the growth achieved was accompanied by great waste and inefficiency, so that more and more investment was required to attain a given increase in national income. Growth, therefore, was sustained only by pushing the rate of investment or accumulation higher and higher. From a rate of 24 percent of the national income during the First Five-Year Plan (1953–1957) this percentage climbed to 33 percent during the period of the Fourth Five-Year Plan (1971–1975) and peaked at 36.5 percent in 1978, a very high rate by any international standard and particularly so for a poor developing country.[2]

Put differently, consumption as a share of national income fell from 76 percent to a low of 63.5 percent, and personal consumption, obtained by subtracting military and other government consumption expenditures from these totals, may have fallen even further. Thus the standard of living of the Chinese people was not growing as rapidly as the country's national income. Real wages per worker in the 1970s were unchanged from the average level of the 1950s. Urban incomes rose, but only because a much higher percentage of urban family members participated in the work force. Real income per farm worker in rural areas fared better, rising at roughly 1.9 percent a year between 1957 and 1978, but this increase was due mainly to the increased prices paid to farmers for their crops, not to substantial rises in agricultural output per worker in constant prices.[3] In short, because of waste and inefficiency, the Chinese people were benefiting only modestly from the economic growth that was occurring. The party and the government kept rising expectations in check partly by not allowing people to read about what was happening to consumption in countries around China.

A second problem with the development strategy of the late 1960s and much of the 1970s concerned the ineffectiveness of the system in producing what was most needed. Steel, for example, was produced in considerable quantity, but certain varieties were overproduced in relation to national need while other varieties remained in short supply.[4] Thus China simultaneously experienced a steady rise in steel imports from under 1 million tons in 1965 to over 8 million tons in 1978, while domestic inventories of steel climbed steadily until they were equivalent to nearly a year of domestic production.

It was the energy sector in which poor planning caused the greatest trouble. Because of the profligate use of energy by Chinese industry, economic growth in the 1960s and 1970s was made possible only by the very rapid development of China's petroleum sector. Were it not for the discovery of the Daqing and Shengli oil fields, China would have had to rethink its development strategy much sooner. As late as 1977, China's planners still believed they could sustain a heavy industry-oriented development strategy by the simple expedient of finding more large oil fields. The ten-year plan that was dusted off and published at that time called for the development of ten new oil fields comparable in size to that at Daqing. Petroleum production was projected to jump from 2 million barrels a day to perhaps as much as 8 or 10 million barrels a day,[5] thereby meeting China's domestic energy needs and providing a substantial surplus for export. But the reality was that not even one new Daqing had been discovered and

China's petroleum production was leveling off at 2 million barrels a day, with little prospect for change until the mid-1980s at the earliest.

Reforms—The First Phase

It is doubtful that China's leaders in the immediate aftermath of Mao's death clearly saw the problems created by the strategy of the past decade. Their dissatisfaction with the status quo in economic affairs may have been triggered by little more than their revulsion at some of the Luddite-style arguments of their leftist critics over the previous decade. They may also have begun to see more clearly that China, far from catching up, was falling further and further behind its East Asian neighbors.

Whatever their reasoning, China's leaders in 1977 and 1978 moved quickly to settle two issues that had been major bones of contention between the left and the right during the previous decade. The left had argued that dependence on foreign trade in general and foreign technology in particular was harmful both to the economy and to other important goals. There was no need for such dependence because China could develop more appropriate technology on its own and could provide for its other needs through domestic production rather than imports.[6] In certain circumstances, of course, such arguments may be valid, but in China in the 1960s and early 1970s they were carried to such extremes that anyone who suggested it might be desirable to import a major new piece of equipment was vulnerable to criticism.

The other economic argument between left and right was over the role of material incentives in encouraging good work performance. Contrary to some popular impressions, China did not eliminate wage differentials during the Cultural Revolution, but most of the incentive features of the wage system were removed. Almost no one was promoted from one wage grade to the next, piece-rate wages and bonuses were eliminated, and no across-the-board wage increases were granted. Labor discipline appears to have broken down in many instances; workers were not dismissed even if they failed to show up at work for weeks at a time.

The issue of the role of foreign trade was settled decisively in 1977 and 1978 in favor of expanding trade. What happened next is illustrative of what often happens in the first phase of a major reform movement when the parties involved understand only the broad outlines of what they are trying to accomplish. In short, there was chaos. Encouraged to think positively about the use of imported technology, Chinese enterprises began to sign letters of intent with abandon. Some informal estimates suggest that hundreds of billions of dollars of imports were tentatively contracted for. Inasmuch as China's foreign exchange earnings were only US$10 billion a year, the country obviously could not have managed to pay for imports of that magnitude. Centralized control over the allocation of foreign exchange was quickly reestablished, and most of the tentative agreements reached were abrogated.

New policies settled the question of material incentives in a relatively decisive way. In the industrial economy, promotions, piece rates, and bonuses were reintroduced. Then in 1978, a general wage increase was granted to a substantial proportion of the urban work force. The large increase in prices paid to farmers had its major impact in 1979 and 1980. By 1980, this across-the-board increase in purchasing power had outstripped the availability of consumer goods on the market, and even the official retail price index rose by 7.5 percent. The real rate of inflation was probably higher. Inflation can be a problem for any government, but for the Chinese it brought back memories of the hyperinflation of the 1940s that had contributed greatly to the Chinese Communist party's rise to power. Hence politics dictated that something had to be done to bring inflation under control.

As these reforms were unfolding and running into more than a little trouble, Deng Xiaoping and the people around him were regaining power and consolidating their position. Chen Yun, in particular, had regained a major role over the management of the economy, and in key provinces, party first secretaries—notably Zhao Ziyang in Sichuan and Wan Li in Anhui—had begun experimenting with even more dramatic reforms.

Faced with chaos in the management of foreign exchange and with rising inflationary pressures a year or two later, a more cautious leadership might have decided to revert to the system it knew best— namely, the command economy it had established with Soviet help. In the early 1960s this, in essence, was what the same leaders had done to restore order following the chaos of the Great Leap Forward. But by the late 1970s, the costs of inefficiency and planning mistakes in the command system were, as earlier noted, becoming increasingly apparent.

The complete political history of this first phase of the reform effort has yet to be written, but by the Third Plenum of the Eleventh Party Congress in December 1978, decisive steps were under way— steps not back but pushing ahead with reform. If imports were desirable in order to accelerate growth, the answer was not to find ways to hold imports down to previous levels but, instead, to look for the means to expand foreign exchange earnings so that the increased imports could be paid for. In a similar manner, rises in wages and in the purchasing power of farmers had to be matched by increases in consumer goods available for purchase.

The logic of this position was further reinforced by the energy crisis that was becoming more and more evident. The year 1978 was the last one in the 1970s to witness a major rise in petroleum output (i.e., by 11 percent). The increase in 1979 was only 2 percent, and production in the next two years fell. Without major increases in energy, an industrial program based on energy-intensive heavy industry could not be sustained. Declining petroleum output meant that foreign exchange would have to be obtained from some source other than expanding petroleum exports. Given the slow growth of agricultural production, exports of manufactured consumer goods became the prime candidate for expansion.

The situation in 1978 and 1979 thus led decisionmakers to agree on a goal of expanding production in the consumer goods industry. In 1979, light industry grew slightly faster than heavy industry, and in the next two years heavy industrial production actually fell, whereas light industry grew by 35 percent. The almost exclusive emphasis on light consumer goods constituted only a temporary palliative, however. Given China's size, a return to something of a balance between heavy and light industry was inevitable.[7] But before that could be made possible, the energy bottleneck had to be broken either through increased production or more efficient use or both.

Increasing International Trade and Exchange

Just as a number of factors pushed China in the direction of a greater emphasis on consumer goods, similar forces pushed the country in the direction of greater involvement with the international economic and scientific system. During the Cultural Revolution, as already indicated, imports of foreign technology were severely restricted. Even domestic research and development activities were sharply curtailed, as scientists were sent to the countryside to learn from peasants, and the universities were closed. The situation in the early 1970s was less restrictive than that in the early 1960s, but restrictive nevertheless.

If China was going to modernize its economy quickly, it could not afford to waste the scientific and engineering talent it did have, and it could not turn its back on the rapid gains to be made through the adaptation of foreign technology. Chinese scientists had had little formal training abroad after 1960 and only limited contact with the international scientific community, and Chinese universities were in a shambles much of the time between 1958 and 1976. A policy of doing nothing to increase the supply of scientific talent meant that what few scientific assets the Chinese had would dwindle and that the prospects for China's economy would be bleak.

The abortive nature of China's initial turn outward in 1977 and 1978, therefore, was not followed by a return to policies characterized by turning one's back on the outside world. To some degree, China could take advantage of the world's accumulated stock of technological knowledge without expending large amounts of foreign exchange. Scientific exchange programs could bring foreign scientists to China at little expense. Universities within China could be put back on their feet and told to concentrate once again on technical training. Student quality was guaranteed by a return in 1979 to rigorous entrance examinations. Research institutes could again receive and utilize international scientific journals. In many ways the most dramatic change in this context was the decision to send thousands of people abroad to upgrade their skills in American, West European, and Japanese universities and research institutes. By 1984, there were 12,000 students and visiting scholars from China in the United States alone, and nearly comparable numbers elsewhere in the West. If China had paid the full cost of these students and scholars, the average annual bill in the early 1980s might have been almost US$500 million.[8] In practice, because Western university charges fell well below any measure of the true cost of visitors and students, and because numerous scholarships, sources of family support, and other special arrangements were available, the actual cost to China was probably well under one-fifth of this amount.

But not all of China's needs could be met by exchanges and education programs alone. To take full advantage of its status as a "follower" country,[9] China had to be able to import technology embodied in machinery and equipment. Furthermore, the advantages of expanded foreign trade involved much more than the importation of technology. Trade allows a nation to put more of its resources into what it does best, into the products in which it has a comparative advantage, and to import those items that can be manufactured only at high cost. Foreign imports can also be used to make up for shortages of products caused by errors in planning.

The lesson of 1977-1978, however, was that China did not have nearly enough foreign exchange to pay for all the imports its plant managers might want to order. China's reformers thus had to find a way to earn more foreign exchange, and from the outset they experimented with virtually every method used elsewhere that had some reasonable prospect of working in China. Many of these experiments started slowly, and critics were often skeptical about whether they would work at all; but, after a year or two of experimentation and false starts, most of the reforms took hold.

Tourism, for example, took a big jump in 1979. Most of this surge resulted from the increasing numbers of visits by Hong Kong and Macao Chinese. But the number of non-Chinese visitors also climbed steadily, and by 1983 foreign exchange earnings from tourism (in *renminbi* [RMB], the Chinese currency) were RMB1.86 billion (approximately US$1 billion), four times the level of 1978.

The People's Republic of China replaced the government of Taiwan in its seats in the World Bank and the International Monetary Fund. Prior to the mid-1970s, China had made a virtue of its complete lack of foreign debt, and the Chinese continued to avoid significant borrowing at high commercial-bank lending rates. But by the mid-1980s, China was borrowing US$1 billion a year from the World Bank, much of it at highly subsidized International Development Association (IDA) rates; it was also receiving subsidized credits from Japan and a number of its trading partners in Western Europe.

The real key to greater foreign exchange earnings, however, was expanded exports. For a quarter century China had lived with a Soviet-style foreign trading system in which all contact with foreigners was handled by corporations attached to the Ministry of Foreign Trade. These corporations stood between the Chinese end user or supplier and the foreign corporation making a purchase or sale. More often than not, the foreign corporation did not even know who the end user of a piece of equipment it was selling would be, or who was supplying the product it was trying to sell abroad. Even if it knew the name of its supplier, the foreign corporation could not work with that supplier to ensure that the product met the style and quality requirements of the foreign market.

This situation began to change in the late 1970s and the change gathered momentum in the early 1980s. In many cases Chinese enterprises began to deal directly with foreign purchasers and suppliers. Individual provinces were given independent authority to promote trade and investment within their territory and to keep a portion of the foreign exchange that resulted. To deal with the special problems of offshore petroleum exploration and development, an area in which China needed both the technology and the capital of the major foreign oil companies, the China National Offshore Oil Company (CNOOC) was formed.

As foreign investment was believed to be one important way of promoting exports as well as a source of foreign technology not available through other channels, a joint venture law was promulgated. At first, the results were disappointing because prospective investors were leery of investing in a country with no legal framework (such as tax laws for foreigners) into which a joint venture might fit. But the early 1980s saw the beginnings of that legal framework, and investors started to make commitments. In the first nine months of 1984, China realized US$1.66 billion in foreign investment, double the level of the same period in 1983, and signed agreements that would lead to another US$1.91 billion in the future.[10] Altogether, 239 new joint ventures were approved in that period.

In a similar vein, China created special economic zones in which foreigners could set up enterprises, hire labor, and import duty-free goods that could be processed and re-exported. The first zones were set up in 1979. Progress was slow at the start, but by 1983-1984, Shenzhen, next to Hong Kong, was beginning to look like an extension of the British colony without the Union Jack. The agreement between China and Hong Kong, reached in 1984, with its emphasis on "one country with two systems," implied a long-term commitment to trade-promoting reforms. It was also in 1984 that the government granted to fourteen coastal cities and Hainan Island some of the rights given to special economic zones.

The best measure of the results of these and other efforts was neither the quantity of foreign investment realized or the number of joint ventures but, rather, the rate of expansion of exports. The relevant figures are presented in Table 2.2. The apparent growth in exports from 1965 to 1978 is something of an illusion resulting from the rapid rise in world prices, which was caused initially by the increase in petroleum prices instituted by the OPEC cartel in 1973. The rate of growth since 1978 has been substantial, however—in real terms as well as in current prices. There was some slowdown in growth in 1983 as a result of the world recession, and the growth rate in 1982 would no doubt have been higher as well in the absence of the recession. Exports in 1984, however, had resumed their rapid climb with a 14.6 percent increase in real terms over the previous year.

Another way of measuring China's trade performance is to compare China's foreign trade ratios with those of other large countries, as is done in Table 2.3. From these data it would appear that China takes as much advantage today of the gains from trade as do many other large nations. Chinese exports as a share of gross domestic product are below the average level, as a share of all large countries, but "large" in this case pertains to all countries with a population above 15 million in 1960. Relative to India, the only nation in the world comparable to China in size, China's export ratio was about the same during the autarkic years of the 1960s, but a quarter or more higher than that of India in the 1980s.[11] More surprising, China's foreign

Table 2.2
China's Foreign Trade

	(1) National Income[a]	(2) Exports	(3) Imports	(4) Foreign Trade Ratios	(5) Foreign Trade Ratios
	(billion yuan in current prices)			(2)÷(1)	(3)÷(1)
1952	58.9	2.71	3.75	.046	.064
1957	90.8	5.45	5.00	.060	.055
1965	138.7	6.31	5.53	.045	.040
1978	301.0	16.77	18.74	.056	.062
1980	366.7	27.24	29.14	.074	.079
1982	424.7	41.43	36.76	.098	.087
1983	467.3	43.83	42.18	.094	.096
1984	548.5	58.06	62.06	.106	.113

[a]National income is calculated according to Marxist definitions and excludes many services included in Gross National Product.

Source: State Statistical Bureau, Statistical Yearbook of China, 1983; State Statistical Bureau, Zhongguo tongji tiyao, 1984; and State Statistical Bureau, "Communique on Fulfillment of China's 1984 Economic and Social Development Plan," March 9, 1985.

Table 2.3
International Comparisons of Foreign Trade Ratios
(Trade as a share of gross domestic product)

	Foreign Trade Ratios	
	Exports÷GDP	Imports÷GDP
All countries ($500 per capita)	.244	.254
Large countries ($500 per capita)[a]	.131	--
India (1965)	.039	.060
Indonesia (1965)	.053	.057
Brazil (1965)	.088	.063
Japan (1965)	.108	.094
United States (1965)	.049	.045
- - - - - - - - - - - - - - -		
China (1965)[b]	.038	.033
China (1982)[b]	.081	.072

[a]Large countries as defined by Chenery and Syrquin for purposes of this analysis are those with a population of over 15 million in 1960.

[b]These figures are different from those in Table 2.2 because the Chinese national income was converted into the Western concept of gross domestic product by multiplying the former figures by 1.2 to take into account services.

Source: H. Chenery and M. Syrquin, Patterns of Development, 1950-1970 (London: Oxford University Press, 1975) pp. 20, 21, 75, 192, 193.

trade ratios were nearly two-thirds of those of Japan in the early 1980s.

Reforms in Agriculture

Foreign trade reforms came first, in a sense, but the reforms that have had the greatest impact on the majority of the Chinese people are those that were carried out in agriculture.

Experiments with rural reforms were under way in a few areas as early as 1978. By 1979 rural free markets, which had existed during the Cultural Revolution but under severe strictures, were once again flourishing. Efforts were also being made to move away from the so-called Dazhai system for setting workpoints in the communes toward a system that paid more attention to relating productivity to income received. Major progress toward reorganizing rural production, however, was not made until after Hu Yaobang and Zhao Ziyang became members of the Politburo in early 1980.

The system introduced was called the "responsibility system"; in practice it covered several different ways of organizing rural work and distributing rural income. In retrospect, the key change was the introduction of household contracts. Under these contracts the individual household was allocated a piece of land for use but not for sale. In exchange, the household was required to meet state quotas for taxes, grain deliveries, and the like, but was allowed to keep whatever it earned over and above those quotas.[12]

Hua Guofeng's removal from office as party chairman and premier eliminated the main source of opposition to the household contract system, but lower-level political cadres were often ambivalent or resistant through 1981-1982. Yet the popularity of the system, combined with subtle but continuous support from the top, led to the rapid spread of these contracts. By 1983, most rural areas were using the household contract system as the main method for organizing the cultivation of agricultural crops. Rural industries were often still under collective control, but, for all practical purposes, collectivization of agriculture had ceased to exist. What remained was not private peasant agriculture, inasmuch as land could not be bought and sold and household actions were constrained by quotas and other measures; but neither was it like the collective agriculture of previous times, under which twenty or thirty families shared responsibility for crop production.

The impact of these reforms on the standard of living in the rural areas was immediate and dramatic. The principal statistical indicators are presented in Table 2.4. As these figures indicate, income grew

Table 2.4
Rural Income and Consumption

	Rural Per Capita Consumption		Rural Per Person Income		Share of Family Income from	
	Current Prices (yuan)	Fixed 1980 Prices (yuan)[a]	Current Prices (yuan)	Fixed 1980 Prices (yuan)[a]	Collective %	Private and Other %
1957	79	96	73	88	59.5	40.5
1965	100	109	107	117	58.9	41.1
1978	132	122	134	145	66.3	33.7
1980	173	173	n.a.	n.a.	n.a.	n.a.
1982	212	203	270	259	52.9	47.1
1983	233	220	310	293	54.7	45.3

[a]There is no available price index for rural consumption goods so these data were deflated by the general retail price index. The size and direction of the bias introduced by using this index is not known.
Source: State Statistical Bureau, Zhongguo tongji tiyao (Peking: China Statistics Press, 1984), pp. 90 and 97.

faster than consumption between 1978 and 1983 (by 102 versus 80 percent), but the increases in both income and consumption were enormous. More was achieved in these areas in the five years after 1978 than in the previous twenty-one years. (Consumption between 1957 and 1978, for example, had risen only 27 percent, or 1.1 percent per annum.)

The figures also show that much of the increase in income resulted from activity outside the collective economy. By 1983, the collective economy accounted for just over half of all farm family income, down from two-thirds in 1978. And the half that was collective presumably included income produced under the household contract system.[13] (It should be noted that the sharp increases in income reported in this table occurred after many reforms had been introduced, but before the household contract system had had much time to take effect.)

The figures in Table 2.4 are national averages. They say nothing about what has happened to the distribution of income. Many scholars in the field expect that the responsibility system will lead to increased inequality, which in turn might create political tensions that could undo the reforms. Certainly some individuals and households have done extremely well, thus eliciting feelings of envy among those who have benefited less. By 1983 and 1984, many urban residents in China were speaking, often with a note of disapproval in their voices, of how rural people were doing better than they were. But the reality was that only the very rich suburban farmers were better off than some urban residents. The great majority of peasants, despite the increases in income since 1978, lagged far behind even the poorer urban people.

It will be years before trends in the rural distribution of income become clear. Whether inequality has increased slightly or decreased since the end of the Cultural Revolution, the evidence seems to indicate that the great majority of China's rural population has received large material benefits from reform. That fact is likely to be more important, in terms of its impact on politics, than the impact of the jealousies aroused. It is hard to disagree with policies that produce that much measurable success. Any future political leader contemplating a return to full collectivization would have to be very brave, strong, and/or foolish to risk imposing major restrictions on individual initiative in the rural areas that might result in a sharp decline in living standards. Even an ardent collectivist, if prudent, might find it wiser to achieve an increase in collectivism through the spread of local industries rather than by forcing households together to raise crops. Economies of scale that exist in industry but not agriculture make the industrial sector a more fruitful area in which to reduce the role of the individual household economy.

Urban Reforms

Experiments with urban reform also began long before the major pronouncement on urban reform by the Twelfth Central Committee at its Third Plenum on October 20, 1984. One early trigger to urban reform was the issue of how to deal with urban unemployment caused by the return to cities of youths "sent down" to the countryside in earlier years. There was no way to absorb all these youths into state enterprises, many of which were already overstocked with workers who had little to do. Therefore, many of these youths were allowed to set themselves up in business as individuals or as members of urban collective enterprises. They opened small restaurants, set up repair shops and other retail outlets, or became pedicab operators. The prestige and security of these jobs may have been low, but the income was often above what could have been earned in the state sector. From the standpoint of the urban consumer, these individual and collective enterprises filled an important gap in urban services. No longer did the state system have a monopoly on such services. Competition from the collective sector was sufficiently strong that state stores were pressured into staying open longer and behaving as though the customer mattered.

Farmers coming into the city to sell their produce played a similar role in expanding the quantity and improving the quality of urban services. There is no way, on the basis of data now available, to measure the impact of these improvements, but it is likely that the quality of urban life was considerably bettered. Through 1984, only suburban farmers, who could come in early in the morning and leave at night, and urban youth could play these roles. The rural population as a whole was still strictly prohibited from migrating to the cities to live. In the five years from 1978 through 1982, for example, the total number of rural people who received urban employment was only 5.05 million. During those same five years, the rural work force grew by 30.3 million from a base that already contained a large number of "surplus" or underemployed rural workers.

The real key to urban reform, however, rests not in the informal or service sectors but in the state-owned enterprises that dominate the urban scene. The progress of reform in this area through 1984 was much slower than that in the rural and foreign trade sectors. There was much experimentation with new rules for enterprise be- havior, particularly in a few key cities such as Chongqing, but the Soviet-style command system of the 1950s and 1960s was still very much intact.[14] On October 20, 1984, however, the Chinese issued a document from the Third Plenum of the Twelfth Central Committee calling for across-the-board reform in the urban sector.[15] Although the document itself is full of ambiguities, analysis of its contents is a useful basis for describing how far urban reforms had progressed by the end of 1984 and how much further they were likely to go in the future. The subject is of central importance because it is the state enterprise sector that will still dominate China's economy in the year 2000 and beyond. Thus, if reforms do not have a major impact on that sector, the impact of reform on the Chinese economy in general will be limited.

The central objective defined in the Third Plenum document is to restore vitality to the nation's million or so urban enterprises by providing each enterprise with a much higher degree of autonomy from central planners and ministries than has existed in the past. But how, in practice, can such autonomy be provided in a Soviet-style centrally planned system? A brief description of the role of the enterprise in a system of central planning will give some indication of how far the government will have to go before anything like real autonomy will be achieved.

In China's Soviet-style system of central planning, the authority to make most major decisions resides with those who draw up the plans (i.e., the members of the Planning Commission) and with the organs whose primary responsibility is to see that the plans are implemented (including the State Economic Commission and the People's Bank). The Planning Commission sets targets on an annual basis for the amount of output required in each industry and the inputs that will be required to achieve that output. These targets are made known to Provincial Planning Commissions and eventually to individual enterprises, which recommend changes so that local conditions are taken into account. These recommendations pass back up through the bureaucracy to the Planning Commission, which balances conflicting claims and sets the final targets. Once set, such targets have the force of law, and enterprises are expected to obey them.

The Chinese, however, do not rely on law alone to keep enterprises in line with the plan. An enterprise can receive the amount of inputs it needs only if the inputs are specified in the plan. The goods must be paid for with money, but no amount of money will ensure an adequate supply of electric power or steel if the plan does not include these factors as input requirements. If the plan does make provision for these inputs, the enterprise can always borrow the funds required from the People's Bank. The Bank, however, is generally not supposed to make loans to finance purchases by enterprises that would be outside the scope of the plan. In fact, the Bank must monitor how the enterprise spends its own money to ensure plan compliance.

Because plans are inevitably imprecise and inaccurate, the system of central planning is not as rigid in practice as it is in theory. If it had been, the Chinese economy would have ground to a halt by now. What little autonomy and flexibility the enterprise possesses, however, has almost nothing to do with the market. For the enterprise, the key objective is to guarantee the supply of inputs it needs to meet its output targets. The first step is to bargain with the planners to get as large an allocation as possible. The next step is to establish formal and informal contacts with other enterprises, not only to guarantee delivery of the goods provided in the plan but also to trade unneeded inputs of one's own for key inputs over and above those in the plan. If an enterprise is allocated inputs that it does not need, it puts them in its warehouse rather than returning them. One never knows when it may be possible to trade that good for another that is useful. Inventories in China, as a result, are typically very large.

Although these bargaining and trading practices introduce some flexibility into the system, they also require that enterprise management spend much of its time negotiating special deals with the government planning bureaucracy and with the managements of other enterprises. A manager skilled at making deals through the "back door" is often in a better position to guarantee the success of an enterprise (i.e., by surpassing the output target) than is one who knows how to organize labor to use inputs more efficiently. And the manager whose only skill is to know how to save money, as opposed to saving electric power or some other input in short supply, is often of little use in achieving success. Money can always be borrowed at negligible interest rates from the People's Bank or be taken out of the enterprise's net income, which the enterprise is not allowed to keep in any case.

The path to greater enterprise autonomy involves the elevation of an enterprise manager from the status of low-level bureaucrat fighting for his or her share of the administrative pie to a position of real independent decisionmaking and power over the future of that enterprise. But one cannot give greater autonomy to enterprises without having some method for coordinating inputs and outputs, and there are really only two ways of achieving such coordination. One is to rely on central planners to balance inputs and outputs; the other is to turn that role over to the market. If neither method is used, as was the case during the Great Leap Forward in China (1958–1960), the result is chaos—factories turning out massive quantities of products without any concern for whether or not a market for those products exists.

The main thrust of the Third Plenum decision is that a much larger share of the task of coordinating China's urban enterprises will be turned over to the market and that the scope for centrally planned coordination will be correspondingly reduced. But converting from central planning to greater use of the market is a complex task involving four major changes in the way the economic system works. All four changes must be carried out in tandem if the market is to play its designated role with some degree of efficiency. By looking at each of these changes in turn, we can get a clear picture of just how far Chinese reforms had come by the time of the Third Plenum decision (October 20, 1984) and how much further they might go if the leadership stays the reform course.

1. If a market is to have any meaning at all for enterprises, inputs to the production process must be available for purchase on that market. This requirement thus implies that a substantial portion of the products that an enterprise produces must be sold on the market rather than delivered to the central authorities for allocation according to the plan. In a separate directive that preceded the Third Plenum decision, the State Council approved a Planning Commission recommendation to cut the number of industrial products subject to "mandatory planning" from 120 to 60. A second category of goods will be subject to "guidance planning," which involves greater use of market controls but presumably still some degree of direct allocation. The 60 products subject to mandatory control outside the market include all energy sources, most metals, basic raw materials for the chemical industry, "important" machinery and electrical equipment, and several other items.

Clearly the central authorities have retained a high degree of direct control over industrial enterprises, and they can exercise this control if they choose to do so. If, on the other hand, the number of products subject to mandatory planning is further reduced in later years, and if many of these products are in part available through market channels, the Chinese will have gone a long way toward market socialism.

2. Simply making goods available for purchase and sale on the market, however, does not create an efficient system of allocation. A second crucial criterion for successful reform is that enterprise managers must respond properly to market signals. If they do not, the result can be a chaotic situation such as that resulting from insufficient control over the importation of foreign goods in 1977 and 1978. At that time, enterprise managers attempted to purchase vast quantities of imports because they had little or no incentive to save foreign exchange. Success for them was determined by surpassing the target for the gross value of output; the more inputs they could accumulate, the easier it would be to expand output.

The key to getting enterprise managers to respond to market signals, therefore, is to compel them to pay more attention to making profits than simply to expanding output. And one way to get them to concentrate on profits is to allow them to keep a larger portion of those profits and to use them for bonuses for themselves and their workers. Until recently, enterprises turned over all of their profits (except for a certain percentage of above-plan profits) to the state budget. The new system calls for each enterprise to turn over profits in accordance with various tax rates set on a more or less uniform basis for all enterprises. Presumably these new Chinese taxes will be something like the corporation and sales taxes in the United States, but in China there may be as many as ten or more kinds of taxes. Furthermore, given the great disparity between rates of profit of enterprises even in a single industry, these tax rates may initially have to be informally adjusted to avoid causing favored enterprises to run at a loss. In the beginning, therefore, the operation of this new tax system may not look very different (from an enterprise director's point of view) from the previous way in which profits were handled. Over time, however, enterprises that succeed in raising profit levels probably will end up keeping a larger and more predictable share than was true in the past.

3. If profits are to be an appropriate guide to enterprise behavior, those profits must be determined by prices that reflect true relative scarcities in the economy. If prices are set incorrectly, and if they do not reflect the real conditions in the Chinese economy, they will give

the wrong signals and enterprises will produce too little of what is in short supply and too much of what is already in surplus.

Major and continual adjustments in prices will be required if the Chinese price system is to play this role. Most prices in China were fixed in the 1950s and have rarely been altered since then. One objective of the Third Plenum decision was to "reform the over-centralized system of price control, gradually reducing the scope of uniform prices set by the state and appropriately enlarging the scope of floating prices within certain limits and of free prices. Thus prices will respond rather quickly to changes in labor productivity and the relation between market supply and demand."[16]

But the Chinese attitude toward price reform is more ambivalent than this statement seems to imply. Many fear that freely floating prices will lead to renewed inflation, which could have grave political consequences. Others do not really understand how markets work and fear the chaos that might result if administrative controls are relaxed in favor of guidance through the price mechanism. In the Third Plenum decision, only two sets of prices—energy prices and agricultural prices (in the latter case, the purchase price is higher than the urban sales price)—were singled out for immediate reform. Moreover, the increase in energy prices is not expected to bring the supply of and demand for energy into equilibrium. Rather, the policy of planned, or administrative, allocation of energy resources is to be retained.

The major question about China's price reform effort, therefore, is whether it will go far enough to have much effect. Zhao Ziyang's announcement on January 1, 1985, that China plans to reduce or abolish delivery quotas for agricultural products suggests that market price setting may become the norm in rural areas,[17] but how far the leadership intends to let the market determine prices in the industrial sector is not yet known. As the agricultural sector has always made substantial use of market forces, enlargement of the scope of market forces there is a comparatively simple task. In the industrial sector, where market forces have had a minor role at best, incremental steps toward increasing that role are much more difficult to achieve.

4. Finally, if increasing the role of market forces is to lead to higher levels of efficiency, enterprises must compete with each other rather than being given monopoly control of particular markets, as has so often been the case in the past. According to the provisions of the Third Plenum decision, "for a long time, people used to consider competition peculiar to capitalism. . . . [Now] our enterprises are put to the test of direct judgment by consumers in the market place so that only the best will survive. This will help to break the blockade

and monopoly hampering the growth of production, lay bare the defects of enterprises quickly, and stimulate enterprises to improve technology, operation and management."[18]

None of the data currently available provide a measure of the degree to which competition between enterprises has increased in recent years. Enterprises appear to be less restricted in terms of where they can and cannot sell. Urban collective businesses are providing real competition for state enterprises in retail trade. And even China's airline, the Civil Aviation Administration of China (CAAC), is being faced with competition from provincial airlines. But as long as central planners allocate key inputs by administrative means, competition will be limited—at least in the market for intermediate products.

Reform leading to a major role for market forces thus has a long way to go in the urban and industrial sectors. Experiments over a number of years have led to a major party decision to push ahead on a national basis, but that party decision contains numerous caveats that could be used by opponents to abort the reforms. Whether the proponents or opponents of reform are likely to win out in the end remains to be seen.

The Future for Reform

In discussing the future of reform in China, it is common to concentrate on the issue of what happens after Deng Xiaoping leaves the scene. Certainly the reforms of the 1977–1984 period would have taken a different and probably more modest course if Deng had not won the struggle for leadership during 1976–1978. The people he then promoted to high positions, notably Hu Yaobang and Zhao Ziyang, have been in the forefront in pushing for continued and often radical reform. The fact that these two reformers already hold the posts of party chairman and premier should put them in a strong position to hold onto these posts even in the absence of Deng. The key party Secretariat is solidly in the hands of reformers, and the Politburo rarely meets (in any case, the influence of the reformers is increasingly dominant there too). Even the senior ranks of the army, widely considered to be a major focus of opposition to the policies of the early 1980s, experienced major changes in leadership in 1984, partly as a result of increased retirements. It is true that many members of the party joined during the Cultural Revolution period and that some of these members can be presumed to have had, and may still have, sympathies for some of the goals of that movement, but it is difficult to see how these people could organize to gain power. The Chinese Communist party is structured in such a way as to prevent such actions from below. Still, when all these considerations are taken into account, no one outside China and probably not many within the country know how politics will work in the post-Deng era. Even if Hu and Zhao retain their positions, they may have to compromise with antireform groups in the army and elsewhere.

But there is more to the future of reform in China than the names of those who hold the top leadership posts. Reform was not the idea of just one or two people at the top; rather, it reflected a widespread frustration with the slow pace of economic progress and improvements in the living standards of the Chinese people. The opening of trade and other contacts with the West and Japan further reinforced these frustrations at many levels. When Deng Xiaoping first visited Japan, pictures of the high living standards of the Japanese were spread across Chinese television and viewed by many millions of people. As more and more information about the outside world poured in, it became increasingly difficult for influential Chinese to ignore the fact that their East Asian neighbors had done far better economically over the past two to three decades.

At the same time that these other East Asian nations were leaping ahead, the Soviet Union's centrally planned economy was experiencing increasing difficulties. In the 1950s, the Soviet Union's economy had been the model for many developing nations, including India as well as China; but in the 1980s it was seen as an economy that, although powerful and still growing, was plagued by increasingly serious waste and inefficiency. Advocates of the advantages of the command economy continued to hold important posts in China, but they could no longer count on unquestioning belief in the efficacy of the Soviet model. The experiences of the Soviet economy in the 1970s and early 1980s suggested that the problems China had encountered in trying to operate a command system were not unique to China but inherent in that kind of system.

In some cases, China's reforms have built up a momentum of their own that would be difficult to reverse, even if the top leadership were to consider doing so. This is particularly the case in agriculture. Even if party leaders still had the power to dismantle the household contract system and return to collectivized agriculture, why would they dismantle a system that had been such a conspicuous success (i.e., in doubling the standard of living of the average Chinese farmer)? If a return to collectivization were to lead to a sharp drop in rural incomes, as is possible or even likely, political as well as economic costs to such a move would be incurred.

The sources of built-in momentum in the industrial sector are more limited than those in agriculture—in part, because progress toward industrial reform has been much more modest than that toward agricultural reform; moreover, few improvements are directly attributable to reform. More significant is the built-in resistance of the bureaucracy that is responsible for implementing the reforms. An increase in the role of market forces means a commensurate reduction in the role of administrative rules and decisions and, hence, a direct loss of power for the bureaucracy. Equally important, the people who run China's economic bureaucracy have been trained to run a command system, and a move toward greater use of the market could make much of this training obsolete.

Still, even in the industrial sector there is some momentum toward reform. The expansion of foreign trade in manufactured goods has made many enterprises conscious of the importance of understanding market forces in general and Western business practice in particular. The influence of Hong Kong can be seen not only in the free-trade zone of Shenzhen next door to Hong Kong but in many other parts of Guangdong Province as well. Elsewhere in China, the command system is being forced to accommodate the rapidly developing small-scale industrial sector. Since 1976, nearly 90,000 new collective industrial enterprises, producing 120 billion yuan in gross output, have been set up in the rural areas and in the suburbs of large cities. In 1983, large-scale enterprises produced only 33 percent of the total net value of industrial output, whereas small-scale enterprises were responsible for 47 percent and medium-scale enterprises accounted for the remaining 20 percent. From the beginning it has been extremely difficult to incorporate these smaller enterprises into a command system. Far from being an insignificant and declining sector of industry, they are large in number and growing.

Clearly, then, economic reform in China is not a slender reed dependent solely on the will of one or two leaders. Nor is it being carried forward by its own unstoppable momentum. Major areas of resistance persist, particularly in the crucial industrial sector, and even the most reform-minded leaders may not know how far they want the process to go. We must wait and see whether the trends in the latter half of the 1980s result in a system that retains key features of the Soviet command model or in one that is quite different.

Notes

1. The statistics used in this essay, except where otherwise noted, are taken from official yearbooks published by China, such as State Statistical Bureau, *Statistical Yearbook of China, 1983* (Hong Kong: Economic Information and

Agency, 1983); and State Statistical Bureau, *Zhongguo tongji tiyao, 1984* (Peking: Statistics Publishers, 1984).

2. For a more detailed discussion of the economics of the Cultural Revolution, see Dwight H. Perkins, "China's Economic Policy and Performance During the Cultural Revolution and Its Aftermath," forthcoming in R. MacFarquhar (ed.), *Cambridge History of China*, vol. 15.

3. These figures represent the national income originating in agriculture per farm worker in current prices; they do not constitute an estimate of personal income. See China Agricultural Yearbook Compilation Committee, *Zhongguo Nongye Nianjian, 1980* (Peking: Agricultural Publishers, 1980), p. 374.

4. Some of the increase in steel imports was due to Chinese needs for varieties of high-quality steel that were beyond the capacity of Chinese enterprises to produce, but China also imported large quantities of those varieties it could manufacture.

5. The ten-year plan did not give a specific target for increases in petroleum production; instead, it specified only the vague "ten new Daqings." The Daqing oil field produced approximately 1 million barrels a day at that time.

6. For a favorable Western analysis of some aspects of this point of view written during the Cultural Revolution, see E. L. Wheelwright and B. McFarlane, *The Chinese Road to Socialism* (New York: Monthly Review Press, 1970), ch. 9.

7. Foreign trade constitutes a much smaller share of national income in very large countries (even those that actively promote foreign trade) than in small countries. Given a smaller trade share, a higher proportion of a country's needs must be met through domestic production. It is difficult, therefore, for such a country as China to specialize in one range of products (e.g., those of light industry) and to import all of its requirements in a major sector (e.g., heavy industry). Foreign exchange earnings are simply not high enough.

8. This figure is a crude estimate based on an average annual cost per student (i.e., for room, board, tuition, transport, etc.) of $20,000. Even this figure understates the average cost of educating a student, but it does include some of the subsidy implicit in the fact that taxpayers subsidize state schools and private donors subsidize the cost of running private schools.

9. This term refers to the advantages of being a follower, rather than the leader, in economic development. Followers can learn from both the successes and the mistakes of the leader and often achieve higher rates of growth as a result. All countries, except for England, were in some sense follower countries in the early period of their growth.

10. *Beijing Review* 27, no. 52 (December 24, 1984), p. 12.

11. India's ratio of exports to GDP has also risen, but only to .052 as of 1980. See United Nations, *Statistical Yearbook for Asia and the Pacific*, 1982, pp. 187, 200. If nonfactor services are included in exports, the ratio in 1980 rises to .070.

12. For a more detailed discussion of the means by which the responsibility system was introduced, see David Zweig, "Context and Content in Policy Implementation: Household Contracts in China," paper presented to workshop,

"Studies in Policy Implementation in the Post-Mao Era, 1977–1983," Columbus, Ohio, June 1983.

13. At this time, we do not know precisely how these figures were estimated, so any statement about what they do or do not include must be treated with caution.

14. A major study of these experiments has been undertaken by a collaborative research team from the World Bank and the Chinese Academy of Social Sciences. See William Byrd, Gene Tidrick, Jiyuan Chen, Lu Xu, Zongkun Tang, and Lantong Chen, "Recent Chinese Economic Reforms: Studies of Two Industrial Enterprises," World Bank Staff Working Paper no. 652 (Washington, D.C.: World Bank, 1984).

15. See "Decision of the Central Committee of the Communist Party of China on Reform of the Economic Structure," adopted by the Twelfth Central Committee of the Communist Party of China at its Third Plenary Session on October 20, 1984 (reprinted in *Beijing Review* 27, no. 44 [October 29, 1984]).

16. Ibid.

17. Zhao made a speech outlining these policies on January 1, 1985. Excerpts appear in *Beijing Review* 28, no. 1 (January 7, 1985), p. 15. He further elaborated his views in an article in *Hongqi*, no. 3 (1985).

18. See "Decision of the Central Committee of the Communist Party of China on Reform of the Economic Structure," October 20, 1984.

3

The Chinese Defense Establishment in Transition: The Passing of a Revolutionary Army?

Paul H.B. Godwin

Introduction

The Chinese leadership and the dominant members of the Chinese military elite see the "modernization of national defense" in very broad terms. Although one of their goals is to improve the current combat effectiveness of the armed forces, this is not their primary focus. Of far greater importance is the development of a defense establishment capable of *sustaining* modern military forces. There is a distinction between simply building forces capable of responding effectively to current needs and creating a defense establishment (including an industrial base) capable of *maintaining* modern military forces and sustaining their requirements for personnel, weapons, and equipment that meet the continually changing technological bases of modern warfare. To achieve the latter objective, a defense establishment must be capable both of fulfilling its own technological requirements without external assistance and of providing professional military education and training that prepares the armed forces to deploy, support, and effectively use the weapons and equipment developed from these technologies.

In this respect, the current goals are similar to those sought in the 1950s, when China was acquiring extensive military technology from the USSR. When the Soviet Union terminated its assistance programs

I would like to acknowledge with appreciation the assistance I have received from Col. Dennis Drew, USAF, of the Air University Center for Aerospace Doctrine, Research, and Education. The views expressed are those of the author and are not to be construed as representing those of the Department of the Air Force, the Air University, or any other agency of the U.S. government.

in 1959-1960, the Chinese defense establishment was unable to sustain a development program sufficiently broad to maintain its military technology at a level comparable to that of the major industrial powers. Most areas of civil technology suffered from the same weakness, which led to the current development program designated the "Four Modernizations."

Defense and the Four Modernizations

As one of the Four Modernizations, the "modernization of national defense" is part of the Chinese leadership's overall objective of bringing China close to the front ranks of the world's leading agricultural, industrial, scientific, and military powers by the year 2000. The defense establishment is viewed by Peking as one of the four major sectors of society that must be brought up to the standards of the world's most advanced states before China will be accepted as one of the globe's major powers. Defense modernization, therefore, is not viewed solely as a response to a particular military threat to China's security, but is seen as part of a much broader pattern of national development. By declaring its intent to rank among the world's leading powers, Peking is also reasserting its quest for autonomy within the international system. The struggle for autonomy, or "independence," within the international system is one of the major underlying purposes of the Chinese revolution and reflects the humiliation that marks the Chinese memory of nineteenth-century imperialism. Military power is viewed as making a major contribution to the autonomy of China.

Nonetheless, defense modernization has been placed fourth in China's scale of investment priorities for achieving the goals of the Four Modernizations. This decision reflects Peking's interpretation of global military and political trends as well as its evaluation of the constraints on defense modernization imposed by China's relatively low levels of industrial modernization and the limited technological sophistication of the society at large.

For the past six years, Peking's leaders, in viewing global military and political trends, have seen no immediate, short-term military threat to China's security. They have felt that the international environment, although turbulent and potentially dangerous, does not pose the kind of military threat that requires China to invest a major portion of its scarce technological and financial resources and its extremely limited base of scientific and technically trained personnel in programs designed to quickly update its conventional forces or accelerate its nuclear weapons program. Furthermore, they have recognized that (1) China's defense industrial base simply could not rapidly absorb (i.e., put to effective use) a massive infusion of advanced military technology and convert it to the serial production of weapon systems sufficient in number to resupply a force structure as large as China's and (2) that China's armed forces lack the technically skilled manpower required to both maintain and use to their best advantage technologically advanced weapon systems and equipment. In short, even if rapid acquisition of such advanced military equipment and technology were seen as desirable and financially possible, neither China's defense industries nor its armed forces are capable of absorbing the technology required to rapidly modernize its defense establishment.

The relegation of defense modernization to fourth priority, however, has not impoverished the defense establishment, for China's estimated defense budget is exceeded only by those of the USSR and the United States. Even now, China's defense-related industrial base is one of the world's largest, producing nuclear-armed ballistic missiles with ranges up to 7,000 miles and the variety of conventional arms usually associated with major military powers. These armaments lack the technological sophistication of those produced by the leading industrial powers; nevertheless, Chinese conventional weaponry has not only been produced in large quantities but has also acquired a reputation for being both rugged and effective. Continued development, production, and deployment of space satellites (including one in geosynchronous orbit), ballistic missiles, nuclear-powered ballistic missile submarines (SSBN), and submarine-launched ballistic missiles indicate that China intends to sustain military programs normally associated with the world's strongest defense establishments. However, China lacks the technological underpinnings required to generate armaments and military equipment utilizing advanced military technology, especially conventional arms; command, control, communications, and intelligence (C^3I) equipment; electronic warfare; and precision-guided munitions (PGMs). Many, if not most, Chinese weapons systems and platforms are based upon Soviet designs and technologies of the 1950s and 1960s.

Defense Modernization Policies

Nothing resembling a long-range defense modernization program has ever been publicly announced in China; however, when new systematic approaches to defense modernization began to emerge in 1978-1979, it soon became evident that a major overhaul of the entire Chinese defense establishment was under way. Commentaries by senior Chinese defense officials and analyses of defense-related issues in China's press and specialized journals all indicated that the "modernization of national defense" was to embrace a wide range of problems, from military doctrine and strategy to the selection, training, and promotion of officers. It also became evident that there were two foci for the policies being developed. On the one hand, the combat effectiveness of the armed forces, using current weapons and equipment, had to be improved. On the other hand, the accomplishment of this objective could not be permitted to delay progress toward the primary objective of creating a defense establishment capable of sustaining modern military forces. The first objective required a major overhaul of the armed forces; the second required a concentration of effort in China's defense industry and in research and development (R&D). The two processes were intimately related; if the People's Liberation Army (PLA) was to become capable of effectively utilizing more sophisticated military technologies when they were introduced in the future, it had to begin preparing for such advanced weaponry and equipment as soon as possible.

As Defense Minister Xu Xiangqian noted in 1979,

> We must admit that our army cannot meet with the demands of modern war. There are many questions concerning the use of modern weapons, the organization of joint operations and bringing the various armed services into play. . . . These are acute contradictions before us and we must make arduous efforts to resolve them. Otherwise, even if our army has advanced weapons, it cannot use them and bring them into full play.[1]

Xu's comments almost certainly reflected the PLA's recent military operations inside Vietnam. In addition, his concern over the inability of the PLA to conduct war successfully on a modern battlefield was reflected in his observation that "we have seen many incidents in the history of war in which an army was defeated, not because its weapons were poor, but because its commander had backward military thinking and directed military operations in the wrong way."[2]

Deng Xiaoping had noted the same problems in 1975, when the party's Military Commission discussed the many weaknesses of the Chinese armed forces; at the time, he had defined a series of problem areas that needed correction.[3] Deng's recommendations to the enlarged conference of the Military Commission in July 1975 could not be converted into policy, however, because of internal power struggles that led ultimately to Deng's dismissal from office in 1976. Even after the death of Mao Zedong in September 1976 and Deng's restoration to power in the summer of 1977, intense internal debates over security policy and the implications of rapid defense modernization for China's overall economic development precluded any systematic approach to the problems faced by the defense establishment.

Then, in 1978, at the Fifth National People's Congress in February and the Third Plenum of the Eleventh Central Committee in December, compromises were made that established a gradual and incremental approach to defense modernization. The threat from the USSR was deemed to be insufficiently dangerous to warrant a massive diversion of resources from civilian to military purposes.[4] China's incursion into Vietnam early the following year and the weaknesses it exposed in the battlefield performance of the PLA served to demonstrate that military technology was not the only source of weakness in the Chinese armed forces.[5] Since that time, the human, organizational, and technological facets of defense modernization have been approached in what appears to be a systematic fashion.

The Short-Term Objective: Improved Combat Effectiveness

Throughout most of the past decade, Deng Xiaoping and others have recognized that the modernization of weapons and equipment is only one part of the complex problem the defense establishment faces as it plans the future of the armed forces. Recruitment and training of officers and enlisted personnel must be radically changed and the tactical training of the conventional forces extensively modified in order to reflect the demands of combat on a modern battlefield. Rapid changes in battlefield technology and the speed and lethality of modern combined arms warfare have made the Chinese leadership sensitive not only to changing tactical requirements but also to the absolute requirement for effective logistical support to sustain forces in intensive combat. China's combat aircraft, artillery, armored fighting vehicles (AFV), and naval combatants, although not as technologically advanced as those of other major military powers, must be properly employed to make the best possible use of their capabilities in battle areas. The Chinese have therefore put a renewed emphasis on the skills and organizational requirements for modern combined arms warfare.

Since 1979, the armed forces have attempted the correction of one of their basic problems—namely, the lack of experience on the part of commanders in dealing with the intricacies of planning and employing combined arms operations. The need for commanders able to maneuver and sustain air and ground forces utilizing diverse weapon systems in swiftly moving battles is now unquestioned. As the Chinese noted in the mid-1970s, when a commander's experience is restricted to light infantry operations and tactics with little use of AFVs, artillery, and airpower, his command capability on a modern battlefield is extremely limited. There is a lack of experience not only among battlefield commanders but also among staff officers planning military operations. At higher levels of command, within the General Staff and General Logistics Departments of the PLA, lack of experience with modern warfare is a major constraint on the overall capabilities of the armed forces. As the minister of defense noted in 1979, contemporary warfare is radically different from the battles fought by Mao's armies in the 1930s and 1940s; to fight a modern war with the methods of past wars would result in sure defeat.[6]

Following initial steps in 1979 to modify the PLA's training exercises, an all-army conference in November 1980 reviewed the previous year's experiences to determine future training requirements.[7] The conference members decided that future training would concentrate on improving the capabilities of the officer corps, and in 1981 Xinhua (New China News Agency) reported that approximately 1,000 commanders were attending advanced courses at PLA military academies. Specifically, they were studying "modern military science," improving their "command skills," and learning about modern warfare through the study of nuclear weapons, guided missiles, electronic warfare, and other aspects of the modern battlefield.[8] Battlefield exercises were concentrating on tank warfare and combined arms operations utilizing air force elements for close air support, air superiority over the battlefield, and battlefield interdiction missions.[9] The high point of the 1981 training year was a massive military exercise involving some 100,000 troops in the largest such operation ever conducted by the PLA. The PLA proclaimed the maneuvers, conducted in the hilly terrain around Zhangjiakou about 100 miles northwest of Peking, to be the turning point in their revised training program.[10]

Later comments on this exercise indicated more precisely its purpose and that of other exercises. A deputy chief of staff noted that they were designed to test the PLA's ability to conduct combined arms operations during the opening phases of a war.[11] The location of major exercises in northern China reinforced the impression that their objective was to prepare the armed forces to block a major Soviet assault before it could penetrate too deeply. Maneuvers undertaken in 1982 continued to reflect this focus on the opening stages of a war, and for the first time tactical nuclear weapons were included in the scenarios. In an exercise designed to train forces to respond to an attack in which battlefield nuclear weapons were used to breach Chinese defenses, paratroops were dropped into defensive positions while helicopters laid antitank mines to impede the enemy's advance.[12] Another large exercise conducted south of the Mongolian People's

Republic was structured around the use of battlefield nuclear weapons to break up a concentration of invading forces. Close air support sorties, air-mobile forces employing helicopter assaults, and tank units were utilized to exploit the disarray created by the use of tactical nuclear weapons in offensive operations.[13]

Simulating the use of tactical nuclear weapons on the battlefield is not difficult; of far greater importance is what the exercises tell us about developments in Chinese concepts of military operations. These exercises clearly indicate that as the PLA gains greater experience in combined arms warfare and in the use of what the Chinese refer to as "composite armies," it is becoming more attuned to the potential role of offensive operations early in a campaign. The concept of "luring" the enemy deep into China and fighting a war of attrition in which his forces are weakened by attacks on his lines of logistical support is being displaced by operations designed to blunt an offensive early in the war.

The emphasis on combined arms exercises continued into 1985, although without any further reports on exercises planned around the use of battlefield nuclear weapons. The PLA did report that the number of combined arms exercises held at the battalion and divisional levels was the highest ever, and that they reflected the changes that had occurred in military training since 1978.

In its efforts to improve the combat effectiveness of its armed forces, the defense establishment has made its priorities clear. The manner in which the PLA now thinks about military operations and trains for war has changed. This change had to occur, and had to become doctrinal, before any major improvements could be made in the PLA's military capabilities. Changes in training have been paralleled by efforts to improve the technical proficiency of the officer corps—a major consideration for an army still led by veterans of the Long March. The defense establishment has taken a careful look at the problems it faces and has begun to implement a set of reforms designed to improve the professional qualities of both the current and future officer corps.

Xiao Ke, the doyen of PLA professional military education and a member of the Long March generation, refers to officer education and training as the "capital construction" of the armed forces. New officers are now selected primarily from among college graduates and graduates of the one hundred or so technical academies and schools specifically created to train a new generation of officers. These PLA-run schools recruit around 10,000 candidates a year from among China's high-school graduates and train them to be "command cadres" and professional and technical personnel. Those few officers selected from the enlisted ranks must attend "command" schools prior to their commissioning and will receive college degrees upon graduation. Within the officer corps as a whole, professional and technical skills are improved through required attendance at the appropriate professional military schools prior to promotion. In the future, officers will not be able to attend advanced schools and academies until they have completed requirements at the lower-level military schools.

These changes have met with extensive resistance, especially from members of the older generation of officers who won their commands in the 1930s and 1940s. Xiao Ke's most bitter comments have been directed at those "comrades who always look back at the past. They even take pride in it. Didn't they command troops and fight past wars despite the lack of culture?"[14] Xiao has observed that, although this was indeed the case in the past, the PLA of the future requires a highly trained and technically competent officer corps skilled in the requirements of contemporary warfare.[15]

The generation of officers too old to function effectively on active duty, especially those unable or unwilling to adjust to the demands of professional training and education now required of the officer corps, is now being encouraged to retire. But convincing these officers to retire has been difficult. In 1983, the PLA chief of staff reported that in combat units, "army" (corps) commanders were approximately fifty years of age and divisional commanders were around forty-five, whereas regimental commanders were below forty.[16] If correct, this report implies that in an army that has long suffered from the influence of a gerontocracy, field commanders now are as young as, if not younger than, their American counterparts at an equivalent level of command. Yet only one year earlier, Deng Xiaoping was complaining that younger officers were not being promoted, especially at the division level.[17]

The severity of the problem of overaged officers is reflected in the benefits offered to members of the old guard to induce them to retire. They are to receive full salary without reduction, an additional one yuan per month for each year served since 1927, and a generous allowance to cover the cost of acquiring a house when they leave government quarters.[18] Despite increasing numbers of reports that senior PLA officers are retiring at the upper levels of command, however, age remains a problem. Xiao Ke in 1983 complained that older commanders were resisting the reforms that require higher education and training levels for officers.

These reforms require centers of professional military education to assume a heavy burden. There are constant reports of expanding curricula containing courses on nuclear weapons, precision-guided munitions, foreign military theories, foreign wars, the history of warfare, electronic warfare, command courses utilizing computers to assist in decisionmaking, and other topics covering all the paraphernalia of modern warfare. Courses stressing contemporary military technology and military operations on the modern battlefield are still complemented, however, by studies of Mao Zedong's military principles and of classical Chinese military thought.

Yet even with all the changes, there is considerable evidence that all is not well in the PLA's centers of professional military education. Constant references to "leftism" inside the military academies were reinforced by a report on an all-army forum on education and training held in November 1983, in which Yang Shangkun of the party's Military Commission complained that old ideas and conventions continued to dominate the curricula. The conclusion drawn at the end of this ten-day conference, attended by senior defense officials, was that many elements of the PLA's professional military education still did not meet the requirements of modern warfare and thus needed to be reformed.[19]

Even though the defense establishment has been stressing since 1979 that the demands of modern warfare and military technology have created an urgent need to retrain the current officer corps, improve the quality of incoming officers, and retire those no longer capable of serving effectively on active duty, problems remained as late as 1983-1984. Given that the opinions of Deng Xiaoping and of the senior officers in the military hierarchy have been expressed with considerable force for almost a decade, we might well assume that resistance to the reforms comes from members of the older generation of officers who are unwilling to see their influence reduced and who may well have serious reservations about the directions the PLA has been taking in recent years. Clearly, the rebuilding of an entire officer corps, especially one so bound by tradition as that of the Chinese People's Liberation Army, is a difficult and conflict-ridden process. Nevertheless, the reforms undertaken since 1978 are important; they represent a change in military philosophy that, when combined with radically revised approaches to military operations, is designed to prepare the armed forces for ongoing revisions in doctrine and strategy.

Doctrine and Strategy: Problems of Transition

Analyses of doctrine and strategy by Chinese leaders and specialists amply demonstrate the connection they see between short- and long-term defense modernization. Both the short-term goal of improving the PLA's combat effectiveness and the development of new doctrine and strategies must fall within the limitations set by China's current military technology.

The doctrinal principles and strategic concepts developed by Mao Zedong in the 1930s provide the appropriate guidance neither for the PLA's current force structure nor for the defense of a China that has undergone thirty-five years of industrial and political development. Xiao Ke defined the problem quite succinctly in 1979, when he observed:

> Now we must study strategy, tactics and military science and technology for waging people's war under modern conditions. To follow the method of "luring the enemy in deep" used by the Red Army during the Jiangxi period and apply it mechanically would be absurd. At that time we occupied no cities and had no modern industry; we took everything we needed from the enemy.[20]

Xiao indicated that the objective of military strategy had changed in the forty-five years since the Red Army fought for its very survival in Jiangxi province. Whereas in the 1930s a major if not primary objective had been simply to preserve the party and the army, in the 1980s the objective was to preserve all that the party had achieved since it came to power. Cities had become "political, economic, and cultural centers and pivots of communication."[21] Furthermore, if China was to use its current force structure effectively, then thousands of combat aircraft, armored fighting vehicles, artillery tubes, and naval combatants had to be sustained with fuel, ammunition, parts, and lubricants. The PLA no longer fought with "millet and rifles," but, even at its current level of modernization, it required extensive logistical support from China's industrial centers. "Luring the enemy in deep," the strategy of the 1930s, could cost China all that it had built since 1949. As Zhang Aiping, the current defense minister, stated in 1983: "The principle of war is to achieve the greatest victory at the smallest expense."[22]

Although "people's war under modern conditions" is the rubric now attached to the modifications made in Mao's doctrinal principles to render them applicable to modern warfare, it is quite evident that these principles are used only loosely as a guide for the development of Chinese military strategy. Indeed, they are used in much the same manner as Clausewitz's *On War* is used by Western military strategists— when it is used at all. Thus, in principle, Chinese strategists accept Mao's concept of "active" or "positive" defense (*jiji fangyu*) as the core of their strategy to defend China against a "future war of aggression." However, precisely what this concept means when applied to strategic nuclear warfare, or to combined arms operations and the use of battlefield nuclear weapons, is another question entirely. The Chinese now refer to their nuclear forces as "strategic nuclear forces"[23] and define their role as one of "counter-strike."[24] Defined in these terms, they perform the now-traditional function of nuclear deterrence by threatening an adversary with a nuclear response to a first-strike. Thus Chinese military strategists have entered the murky realm of deterrent strategies for nuclear conflict. The development of submarine-launched ballistic missiles (SLBM) and nuclear powered ballistic missile submarines (SSBN) demonstrates a concern over the survivability of their retaliatory force, again indicating an orientation toward deterrence and nuclear warfighting that has become "normal" for nuclear powers.

When these developments are combined with observations from high-ranking officials that "without advanced weapons and equipment, we shall pay a higher price and prolong the time for winning a war,"[25] it becomes clear that protraction and attrition will be used as the basis for a strategy only if a protracted struggle becomes absolutely necessary. Chinese military exercises, and their own definitions of what these exercises are designed to achieve, demonstrate that the new doctrine and strategy emerging in China are designed specifically to avoid a protracted war.

This is not to say that Chinese strategists will simply ape Western military thought. China's geopolitical location, climate, and terrain, and the nature of its adversaries as well as the state of China's military technology, will be the primary influences on the strategic concepts they develop. Nonetheless, "the current situation is a bridge joining the future."[26] Moreover, there is some historical experience that the dominant elements in China's military leadership do not wish to repeat. Protracted people's war is part of that experience. Current analyses of doctrine and strategy, when combined with the field exercises conducted over the past five years, demonstrate that the current Chinese leadership sees the development of modern nuclear and conventional forces as essential to the defense of China as well as to its future status in the international system.

The Chinese have answered a question this author posed some three years ago: "Put simply, what happens if the Chinese hold a people's war and nobody comes?"[27] They have no intention of holding one!

A weak link in this emerging strategy and the doctrinal principles underlying it concerns the arms and equipment of China's conventional general purpose forces—a point made with great frequency by China's senior military officials. Twenty years of developments in military technology have passed China by. The long-term goal of defense modernization is specifically directed at creating a research and development (R&D) and industrial base for defense capable of correcting this weakness and preventing its recurrence in the future.

The Long-Term Objective:
A Self-Sustaining Defense Industrial Base

The Chinese learned a very hard lesson in 1959-1960, when the USSR terminated its assistance to Peking's nuclear weapons program and severed its support for the Chinese conventional arms industries. China had been the recipient of a massive defense-technology transfer from Moscow, and future defense programs were based on the assumption that Soviet assistance would be continued. Termination of Russian support threw the defense industries into chaos.

The current long-term defense modernization programs are specifically designed to prevent such a condition of dependence from ever occurring again. Peking is quite confident that, in the long run, a defense R&D and industrial base capable of supporting Chinese military requirements independent of foreign sources of technology can be built. In part, this confidence stems from the success China has achieved in its strategic weapons and space programs, which were developed without extensive foreign assistance beyond the foreign training of certain Chinese who were, in fact, critical to the programs. But, the Chinese also recognize that the success of these programs requires a commitment to concentrate scarce human and technological resources on a particular goal.[28] As a result, in part, of this concentration of effort, conventional weapons and equipment did not advance as quickly as the nuclear weapons, and in this area the Chinese remain largely dependent on outdated designs and technologies. Even now, there are no signs that conventional arms are receiving the emphasis granted nuclear weapons in the past, but since 1978 defense R&D and the defense industries have been overhauled in such a way as to make them both more efficient and less of a burden on the civil sector of the economy. The overall objective of these reforms is to improve the development and production of modern weaponry and equipment and to reduce their cost.

The late 1970s and early 1980s witnessed the introduction of reforms intended to reduce significantly the isolation of defense R&D and production from the civil economy. Changes in the management of defense R&D were designed to minimize the basic problem of coordination created by the large number of organizations involved in the research and development of weapon systems and equipment, and to lessen the general level of waste and inefficiency created by past failures to coordinate related programs carefully. Equally important, developments in defense and civilian R&D programs were to become mutually beneficial through increased coordination and joint planning. Because of critical shortages of trained personnel and facilities, the lack of coordination resulted in waste and partially offset gains from the freedom provided by decentralization.[29]

Increased centralization of defense R&D and production followed in 1982, under the auspices of a newly created Commission in Charge of Science, Technology, and Industry for National Defense (CCSTIND). This organization was placed under the joint supervision of the Military Commission's National Defense Industrial Committee and the State Council's Science and Technology Leading Group (formed in 1983). The CCSTIND was designated the "leading organ for the unified management of the work of modernizing weapons and armament."[30]

While these changes were under way in the supervision and management of defense R&D and production, the leadership of the defense industries was transferred from military to civilian personnel during the period 1978–1982. Previously, the defense ministries of machine building (MMBs) had been numbered (i.e., the Second Ministry through the Eighth), and their responsibilities were officially secret, even though they had expanded their products to include goods destined for the civil economy. Now, they were named (e.g., the Fourth Ministry of Machine Building became the Ministry of Electronics Industry) and their plans for expansion to include civil product lines were made public.

Two factors impelled the reform of the defense industries. First, the removal of the defense MMBs from the exclusive control of the defense establishment and their placement under civilian ministers with the responsibility of producing civilian product lines would reduce the defense industries' burden on the economy. Second, as was widely recognized, the generally superior technology associated with the defense industries could profitably be applied to civil production.[31] Thus began a process of internal technology transfer that should be highly beneficial to the civil sector of the economy. Moreover, internal technology transfer is reciprocal; technologies initially imported for civil applications can also be transferred to the defense sector more easily than in the past.

Through these reforms, Peking is seeking to reduce the unnecessary barriers separating defense and civil R&D programs, defense and civil industrial production, and overall R&D programs and the industrial production they support. Assuming that the efficiencies sought are actually achieved, and that the new defense R&D management system does in fact permit the defense establishment to settle on particular weapons programs and move swiftly toward their completion, is it possible to predict how successful the program is likely to be? Current plans call for the importation of selected defense technologies embodied in weapons systems and equipment such as precision-guided munitions, radars, communications equipment, and so on. These imports will supply defense R&D facilities with samples of advanced armaments and provide the defense industries with experience in the serial production of weapons and equipment based on advanced technologies. Such armaments and military equipment will be selected on the basis not only of their contribution to the current needs of the armed forces but also of the extent to which they fill gaps in the knowledge required for ongoing and planned defense programs. Currently, the defense R&D programs are emphasizing electronics,[32] which form the heart of precision-guided munitions of all types, communications systems, target acquisition systems, and all forms of contemporary armaments.

This emphasis on electronics does not constitute an isolated case; it is an example of what the defense establishment seeks to achieve by focusing on "key" areas of development. Senior defense officials have consistently stated that China will import selected advanced military technologies in order to provide models for future weapons, but that if China is to achieve a level of parity with the military technology of major world powers, it must develop its own scientific and technological capabilities.[33] Thus, imported technology is seen as a catalyst in the development of China's own R&D capabilities. The catalytic effect will not be random, however; it is intended to dovetail with the Chinese defense establishment's own projects. Presumably, as the defense R&D and production facilities gain more experience with advanced technologies, and as increasing numbers of technical and scientific personnel are trained abroad, China's capabilities to develop its own technologies and apply them to weapons and equipment will increase. The Chinese themselves recognize that this will be a slow process. As of now, there is no indication that the armed forces will see a rapid expansion of the technological base of their weapons. Rather, the Chinese refer to the "coexistence of outmoded and modern equipment and of ordinary and advanced technology."[34]

Retrospect and Prospect

The Chinese defense establishment realizes that the task before it is a long-term, broad, and complex one. Although its own analyses indicate that it faces severe problems and significant resistance to the path it has selected, the Chinese military elite knows where it wants to go. The basic strategy for modernization has indeed been established.

The attainment of long-term objectives will have an important effect on China's future role in the international system. But a major overhaul of the armed forces, the defense R&D base, and the defense production facilities is essential to the achievement of these objectives. This the Chinese know only too well. Hence the current situation is one of transition in which the defense establishment has accepted the fact that it cannot correct all of its weaknesses in a few years.

Policies associated with the short-term objective of rapidly improving the combat effectiveness of current forces supply a critical link with the long-term objective. The reforms of officer selection, training, professional military education, and promotion will prepare the officer corps to command and staff future armed forces. Because progress toward armed forces that are modern by the standards of major military establishments will be slow, retiring or retraining senior and middle-ranking members of the officer corps can be undertaken without the disruption created by the dismissal of thousands of senior officers. Issues of reorganization can be reviewed and implemented more slowly than would be the case if rapid change were sought. Basic problems of doctrine and strategy—always potential sources of conflict in any defense establishment—can be worked out without undue haste, and roles and missions can be defined for the service arms and branches over time. Analyses can be made of specific Chinese needs related to the size of the country, its geopolitical location, and its potential defense requirements. Comparisons to foreign defense postures can be drawn, and long-range choices can be made in such a way as to evaluate China's particular needs against the experiences of other military establishments. The short-term goals will permit the adjustments initially required by current military technology to be modified as Chinese weapons and equipment turn the PLA into a more effective battlefield force.

The reduction in the size of China's forces, now under way, is an example of an adjustment being made to fit long-term objectives. This reduction has been accompanied by the creation of a reserve force of officers, which was instituted in part by the establishment of a Chinese equivalent of a college ROTC program and is capable of being called to active duty in times of national emergency. The militia system, already extensively modified since its creation in the late 1950s, will ultimately be entirely merged into the reserve system contemplated by the new Military Service Law.[35] Patterns already established indicate that, over the next decade or so, the Chinese reserve system will function very much like the ready reserves of other major military powers.

Indeed, if the current pattern of defense modernization endures for the next fifteen years, the Chinese defense establishment will present a much different image from the one it now projects. It will not be deploying armaments and equipment that represent the cutting edge of military technology and, in this regard, will still remain "behind" the defense establishments of the major industrial powers. But its armed forces will have weapons with significantly improved range, accuracy, and speed. Its strategic weapons will be greater in number, more accurate, and more survivable than those in its current forces, and its officer corps will be more competent in the skills required to sustain, maintain, deploy and employ the forces.

It is difficult to predict to what extent the continuing gap between Chinese military technology and that of the principal military powers will limit Peking's ability to use its military forces to achieve its political objectives and increase its autonomy in the international system. What does seem evident, however, is that the gross disparity between China and its primary adversaries is coming to an end. If this is the case, then other less tangible factors influencing the outcome of war may become increasingly important. Leadership, strategy, tactics, and mass and unit cohesion will become increasingly significant as military technology becomes less of a distinguishing characteristic separating contending armed forces. These issues involve areas of analysis not addressed in this chapter, but they may well form the basic questions for the next stage of inquiry into the Chinese defense establishment. If so, it is worth recalling not only that the soldiers of the Chinese People's Liberation Army have earned a well-deserved reputation for dogged courage in the face of extreme adversity, but also that Chinese military thought has a tradition of ingenuity perhaps unmatched by the West.

Notes

1. Xu Xiangqian, "Strive to Achieve Modernization in National Defense," *Hongqi* [Red Flag], no. 10, October 2, 1979, in *Foreign Broadcast Information Service, Daily Report: People's Republic of China* (hereafter *FBIS-CHI*), no. 203, October 18, 1979, p. L16.

2. Ibid., p. L15.

3. Deng Xiaoping, "Speech at an Enlarged Meeting of the Military Commission of the Party Central Committee" (July 14, 1975), *Deng Xiaoping Wenxuan* [Selected Works of Deng Xiaoping], Peking, July 1, 1983, in Joint

Publications Research Service (hereafter JPRS), *China Report*, no. 468, October 31, 1983, p. 19.

4. For a thorough analysis of the debate over defense and security issues for the years 1973–1978, see Harry Harding, "The Domestic Politics of China's Global Posture, 1973–1978," in Thomas Fingar (ed.), *China's Quest for Independence: Policy Evolution in the 1970s* (Boulder, Colo.: Westview Press, 1980), pp. 93–146.

5. For a careful analysis of these operations in Vietnam, see Harlan W. Jencks, "China's 'Punitive' War on Vietnam: A Military Assessment," *Asian Survey* 19, no. 8 (August 1979), pp. 801–815.

6. Xu Xiangqian, "Strive to Achieve," p. L16.

7. Peking Domestic Service, November 21, 1980, in *FBIS-CHI*, no. 229, November 25, 1980, pp. L24, L25.

8. Peking, Xinhua (New China News Agency) Domestic Service, January 15, 1982, in *FBIS-CHI*, no. 012, January 19, 1982, p. K5.

9. Peking, Xinhua Domestic Service, January 17, 1982, in *FBIS-CHI*, no. 012, January 19, 1982, p. K11.

10. Michael Weisskopf, "China Reveals Military Maneuvers, Believed Largest in 30 Years," *Washington Post*, September 27, 1981, p. 29; and "Make Fresh Contributions to the Modernization of National Defense" (editorial), *Jiefangjun Bao* (Liberation Army Daily), September 20, 1981, in *FBIS-CHI*, no. 187, September 28, 1981, pp. K2–K3.

11. Peking, Xinhua Domestic Service, January 17, 1982, in *FBIS-CHI*, no. 012, January 19, 1982, p. K11.

12. Peking, Xinhua, July 20, 1982, in *FBIS-CHI*, no. 141, July 22, 1982, pp. K2–K4.

13. *Ningxia Ribao* (Ningxia Daily), June 27, 1982, in *FBIS-CHI*, no. 129, July 6, 1982, pp. K19–K20; and "China Tests New Military Strategy," *New York Times*, July 14, 1982, p. 3.

14. Peking, Xinhua Domestic Service, February 22, 1983, citing a *Jiefangjun Bao* article by Xiao Ke dated February 22, 1983, in *FBIS-CHI*, no. 037, February 23, 1983, p. K31.

15. Ibid.

16. Zhu Ling, "China's Army Is Gearing Itself for Modern Warfare," *China Daily* (Peking), June 11, 1983, in *FBIS-CHI*, no. 114, June 13, 1983, p. K30.

17. Deng Xiaoping, "Speech at a Meeting of the Military Commission of the CPC Central Committee" (July 4, 1982), *Selected Works of Deng Xiaoping* (Peking, July 1, 1983), in *FBIS-CHI*, no. 145, July 27, 1983, pp. K9–K10.

18. "Deng Xiaoping's Arrangements Completed: Military Organs to Be Streamlined," *Ming Bao* (Hong Kong), March 22, 1982, in *FBIS-CHI*, no. 059, March 24, 1982, p. W4.

19. Peking, Xinhua Domestic Service, November 20, 1983, in *FBIS-CHI*, no. 225, November 21, 1983, p. W4.

20. Peking, Xinhua Domestic Service, September 9, 1979, in *FBIS-CHI*, no. 176, September 10, 1979, p. L15.

21. "Nieh Jung-chen's (Nie Rongzhen) 4 August Speech at the National Militia Conference," Peking, Xinhua Domestic Service, August 7, 1978, in *FBIS-CHI*, no. 154, August 9, 1978, p. E7.

22. Zhang Aiping, "Several Questions Concerning Modernization of National Defense," *Hongqi*, no. 5, March 1, 1983, in *FBIS-CHI*, no. 053, March 17, 1983, p. K2.

23. "Deputy Chief of the General Staff Zhang Zhang Talks About the Armed Forces," *Liaowang* [Outlook], no. 31, July 30, 1984, in *FBIS-CHI*, no. 163, August 21, 1984, p. K18.

24. Ibid., p. K20.

25. Yang Shangkun, "Building a Chinese-Style Modernized Armed Force," *Hongqi*, no. 15, August 1, 1984, in *FBIS-CHI*, no. 163, August 21, 1984, p. K11.

26. Ibid., p. K15.

27. Paul H.B. Godwin, "China's Defense Modernization: Of Tortoise Shells and Tigers' Tails," *Air University Review* 33, no. 1 (November-December 1981), p. 12.

28. Zhang Aiping, "Several Questions," p. K5.

29. "Liu Da, Bai Jiefu and Other Deputies (to the 5th National People's Congress) Say that There Must Be an Organ that Coordinates Scientific Research Work," *Renmin Ribao* [People's Daily] September 7, 1980, *FBIS-CHI*, no. 180, September 15, 1980, p. L12.

30. Peking, Xinhua Domestic Service, February 23, 1983, in *FBIS-CHI*, no. 044, March 2, 1983, p. K5.

31. "Zhang Aiping Calls on All Departments of Military Science and Technology and Defense Industry to Help Boost China's National Economy," *Jingji Ribao* [Economics Daily], August 8, 1983, in *FBIS-CHI*, no. 157, August 12, 1983, p. K1.

32. Peking, Xinhua Domestic Service, March 1, 1984, reporting the results of a national conference of directors of electronics industry departments and bureaus that concluded on March 1, 1983, in *FBIS-CHI*, no. 045, March 6, 1984, p. K27.

33. See, for example, Zhang Aiping, "Several Questions," p. K5; and Yang Shangkun, "Building a Chinese-Style Modernized Armed Force," p. K11.

34. Yang Shangkun, "Building a Chinese-Style Modernized Armed Force," p. K11.

35. See "Step Up the Building of the Armed Forces to Defend the Socialist Motherland" (report), in which Chief of the PLA General Staff Yang Dezhi answers reporters' questions on the military service law, *Zhongguo Qingnian Bao* [China Youth], May 24, 1984, in *FBIS-CHI*, no. 108, June 4, 1984, p. K13.

4
Intellectuals and Cultural Policy After Mao

Perry Link

The role of literary intellectuals, especially better-known writers of fiction, drama, poetry, essays, and literary criticism, is extremely important in Chinese society. Although members of the literary elite are a very small fraction of those covered by the Chinese word for intellectuals—*zhishifenzi*, which includes scientists, engineers, teachers, librarians, journalists, (and, when used in its broadest sense, even all high-school graduates)—the literary elite is very influential. Major political and social debates in the People's Republic have been held in the literary sphere and sometimes have originated there. Moreover, contemporary fiction has a tremendous number of readers. Bestsellers are printed in the millions of copies, and surveys show that urban workers read contemporary fiction nearly as much as they watch television and movies.[1] Writers in China can become celebrities on the scale of film stars or professional athletes in the United States. This "star" phenomenon is new; basically, it is the result of greater printing capabilities and rising literacy rates in recent decades. It does not, however, fully reveal the conscious self-conception of writers. For that, one must look to Chinese tradition.

The Role of the Writer

Writers in the People's Republic have always been concerned with national politics—often by preference, but at times out of necessity. It is natural, and correct, to attribute this preoccupation in part to Mao's policies, beginning with his famous "talks" at Yan'an in 1942, when he declared that literature must support the political goals of the state. More fundamentally, though, it is important to bear in mind that ties between writing and politics are centuries old in China. However "modern" writers may be in their language, manner, and conscious ideologies, some of their most basic assumptions about what their relationship to the state should be and about how they should play their social roles are embedded so deeply in their culture as to be beyond question, or even beyond notice.

Briefly stated, four of these basic assumptions are as follows:

Written Chinese embodies moral and political power. Mastery of classical learning, in the famous formulation of the Confucian classic, *The Great Learning*, results in cultivation of one's own self, which, in turn, results in harmony within one's family, regulation of the kingdom, and pacification of the world.[2] Ultimately, literary cultivation qualifies and enables one to rule, or at least to advise a ruler.[3]

A literary intellectual should take the world's well-being as his own responsibility. His learning gives him not only a special power but also a strict moral duty to care whether all is well in "the world" (conceived of as *tianxia*, or "all under heaven," in classical texts; and as the nation of China in modern times). In the famous words of Fan Zhongyan (A.D. 989–1052), the literary intellectual should "be the first in the world to worry about the world, and the last in the world to take part in its pleasures."[4] C. T. Hsia, in his keenly perceptive overview of modern Chinese fiction, chooses "Obsession with China: The Moral Burden of Modern Chinese Literature" as his title and theme.[5]

The literary intellectual has reason to expect that the state will, or at least should, utilize his talents. Through all the great changes that have occurred in the ways in which people of learning have been identified in China—from the "selection of worthies" in the time of Confucius through the system of "recommendation" in the Han Dynasty and Six Dynasties, to the civil service examinations of the latter dynasties—two guiding assumptions have persisted: that the best people should be found, and that their talents should be used for the benefit of the country.

If for some reason one is not appreciated or used, one retires and awaits a better time. In retirement, a writer might commune with like-minded people, or even plot a comeback, cleaving to his ideals but not engaging in explicit public dissent. Brilliant literati such as Qu Yuan (343–289 B.C.) and Jia Yi (201–169 B.C.), who, unappreciated by their princes, languished in exile until their deaths, nonetheless remain cultural heroes because of their loyalty to the ideal of patriotic service. Among modern figures, the pattern appears in the famous writer Lu Xun, who withdrew from government in the chaos of the decade after 1911 to "copy ancient inscriptions" in his hometown.[6] Even Chiang Kai-shek, a man who was almost purely a military and political leader, withdrew to his hometown in 1927 and again in 1949 in accordance with this proud tradition of the intellectual whose words are not heeded.

Four brief points cannot, of course, summarize one of the world's longest cultural traditions, but they do shed an important light on the behavior of intellectuals in the People's Republic. Chinese intellectuals today also assume that power and morality inhere in the Chinese written language; that it is their duty, as intellectuals, to speak from their consciences on important questions facing the country; that leaders of the state ought to heed and respect them; and that, when they are not properly appreciated, their proper course is to withdraw. The withdrawal syndrome, widely apparent through the tumultuous Communist campaigns of the 1950s and 1960s, has appeared in the post-Mao period as well. During the "spiritual pollution" crackdown in the autumn of 1983, many intellectuals developed real or feigned illnesses. Withdrawing from the fray, they "ran low fevers" (*fadishao*) and "wasted away from within" (*neixiaohao*). A year later, when political conditions were much improved, they reemerged.

The Relaxation of Control After Mao

The most important "cultural reform" in the post-Mao period, strictly speaking, has been a reform not of culture itself but of cultural *policy*—specifically, the dramatic relaxation of controls on cultural expression. To be sure, occasional moves have been made to retighten control, and then further steps taken to relax it again, but the major overall trend since Mao's death has been toward relaxation. Most of the other issues that have arisen are wholly or partly a result of this change of policy. (The reason it is important to distinguish reform of cultural policy from reform of culture itself is that the former is within the power of the political leadership whereas the latter is not. Chinese culture, at both the elite and the popular levels, has been remarkably resistant to consciously designed reform.)

It is impossible to say with certainty what brought about the major relaxation of controls. Deng Xiaoping and his allies, who have been primarily responsible for it, have not spelled out all of their reasoning. One can, however, infer a number of likely reasons, based upon the partial explanations that the leaders have offered as well as upon the way in which policy has developed.

First, a relaxation of controls was necessary to "heal the wounds" inflicted during the Cultural Revolution. Political discussion of culture in China commonly employs medical metaphors: Good works of literature and art are "healthful"; bad ones can be "poisonous." The Communist party, implicitly standing in the doctor's role, has traditionally taken responsibility to decide what tonics should be prescribed. After the Cultural Revolution, what Chinese society needed was a healing of the wounds, and literary works that addressed the ills of the Cultural Revolution accordingly began to appear in late 1977. They came to be known, significantly, as "scar" literature.[7] Some of these works, more than mere healing salves, were likened to purgatives, flushing the ill humors of the Gang of Four—or even to the surgeon's scalpel, knifing into the social organism to expose hidden disease.[8] It is difficult to say how many of these "scar" works had the blessings of top leaders. But it is clear that some of them were kindly regarded, and that the leadership had made a judgment that "healing" was important and could not happen without a relaxation of controls.

Second, a relaxation could help to win popular support for the post-Mao regime. This was true not only for the obvious reason that nearly all producers and consumers of culture (writers, readers, opera-lovers, film-goers, and others) like a cultural thaw because of the variety it brings. It was also clear that the content of uncontrolled expression would basically favor the new leadership. The vast reservoir of pent-up resentment about the Cultural Revolution was obvious. To tap it would lend legitimacy to the new leadership and strengthen its mandate for the major policy changes it was planning.

Third, a relaxation of controls could win the confidence of people whose cooperation was essential to the success of the new modernization drive. Two groups of such people were most important. One consisted of scientists and engineers, who obviously were indispensable. As with all other intellectuals, they had been seriously alienated from the party during the Cultural Revolution. (It is true that a few scientific and engineering intellectuals, such as the designers and builders of nuclear weapons and the personal physicians to top leaders, had enjoyed special privileges even during the Cultural Revolution; but they were a tiny minority, and privileged treatment did not extend to all scientists.) The blanket tarring of all intellectuals during the Cultural Revolution was still a fresh memory in the immediate post-Mao years; it would have been impractical for the leadership to turn to scientists and engineers with an exhortation to join the "New Long March" toward modernization while continuing to persecute writers. For their part, scientists in the late 1970s were as assiduous as anyone in defending the slogan "Let a Hundred Flowers Bloom," which called for toleration in cultural matters.[9]

The second group, equally crucial and perhaps even more prob-lematic, were educated youth. Clearly, the achievement of modern-ization by the year 2000 would depend on them. But perhaps no major social group emerged from the Cultural Revolution more cynical than they. There was a serious generation gap between them and the aging leaders, whom young intellectuals tended to view as doctrinaire old men. It thus became very significant that most of the hard-hitting works of social criticism in the post-Mao period were written by *middle-aged* authors (aged 40–55). These authors were old enough to have been influenced by the revolutionary optimism of the late 1940s and early 1950s, and thus to be basically committed to the ideals of the revolution; yet they were still young enough to win the respect of youth. As perhaps the *only* nationally famous people generally admired by youth, they were, from the leadership's point of view, a crucial bridge to the younger generation. To alienate them would have been extremely costly; but to keep them happy, a liberal cultural policy was necessary.

Fourth, Chinese leaders are aware that a relaxation of controls on culture can make a good impression on foreigners and Overseas Chinese. Ironically, the leaders' sensitivity to foreign opinion has been clearest when they have announced crackdowns on intellectuals. Hu Yaobang, explaining the dangers of "bourgeois liberalism" in 1981, predicted that the new policy would inevitably bring criticism from "people both inside and outside China."[10] Others expressing official policy hoped that "foreign friends would realize that China was not reverting to the "campaigns" of the Cultural Revolution and before, but merely exercising the right of "literary criticism."

Why such sensitivity to foreign opinion? Is it warranted? The hearts and minds of Overseas Chinese are, of course, considerations important to China's "united front" policy and its assertion of sovereignty over Hong Kong and Taiwan. It is true, moreover, that Overseas Chinese look to cultural policy as a sensitive indicator of Peking's intentions. But the leadership's concern about non-Chinese foreign opinion clearly seems exaggerated. When foreign banks and businesses question the safety of their investments, they seldom look to cultural policy for answers. Western intellectuals, for their part, have yet to develop a concern for their counterparts in China to match that directed to their counterparts in the Soviet Union. Nevertheless, Chinese attention to foreign opinion remains considerable. Not only Chinese leaders but also writers, editors, performers, and many others assume that foreigners are aware of China's cultural policies and have important opinions about them. The age-old assumption that Chinese culture has something uniquely valuable to offer the rest of the world, combined with the sense that this offering had been stifled completely during the Cultural Revolution, has made it natural to assume that the world is now eagerly watching trends in Chinese culture.

Fifth and finally, we must recognize that not all advocacy of cultural relaxation is as instrumental as the four preceding reasons might suggest. At least some of the top leaders (to judge from the writings of authors who apparently speak for them)[11] regard cultural creativity as enlightened Marxism—worthwhile for its own sake. This view not only conceives free expression as a part of the ideal Marxist society of the future; it also holds that, even in the present, free expression can have the salutary effect of exposing "errors" in policy. The more that opinions "contend," the likelier it is that the "correct" answers will emerge.[12]

As noted earlier, any list of reasons for the relaxation of control necessarily requires an estimate of private (and politically sensitive) thoughts of the top leaders. A certain element of speculation is thus inevitable. But whatever the reasons for the relaxation, its major consequences are empirical and evident enough. The status of "professional writer" was restored, as were manuscript fees, royalties, and other financial benefits for writers. Perhaps most important, the party promised to end the use of "campaigns" as a method of literary control. Writers would no longer arbitrarily be tagged with labels like "counterrevolutionary" or "antisocialist," or be given political punishments for "incorrect thought" (although "literary criticism," which usually carries political overtones, would still be allowed). All these changes were basically in place by the end of 1979. They have been consolidated in the years since then—albeit not always smoothly. The Maoist slogan "Literature Must Serve Politics" was abandoned in the summer of 1980 after a lengthy debate and replaced by a carefully wrought, if vaguely expressed, compromise: "Literature Must Serve the People and Serve Socialism." The new slogan meant that not all writing had to support current political goals, as under the old slogan, but neither could any writing go against "the interests of the people and socialism." In other words, there now was an acceptable apolitical area between support of and opposition to policy. In 1981 the word *freedom* took a beating in the campaign against "bourgeois liberalism"; but in December 1984 the phrase *creative freedom* not only received the party's stamp of approval but was declared to have been correct Marxism all along.[13]

The Expanded Scope for Creativity

From the point of view of the creative artist, the major result of the relaxation of controls is that one can deal with a wider range of topics and ideas, using a greater variety of techniques. Traditionally, writers in the People's Republic have been expected to follow a "road."

While it is true that Chinese writers and thinkers well before the Communist period used this metaphor to symbolize their hope for a "way out" of China's modern historical crisis, the "road" (*daolu*) in the 1950s and 1960s took on a singularity based on an arbitrary concept of "correctness," and thus became oppressive. Moreover, its direction frequently changed. In 1979 a young poet wrote:

> I've walked no end of roads—busy ones, dull ones,
> grim ones, pale ones. I've had enough of roads.[14]

During the post-Mao relaxation, the circle has become a better metaphor than the straight-line road for the expanding limits on expression. The scope of safe topics has widened dramatically, notwithstanding temporary contractions along the way in the form of campaigns against "bourgeois liberalism" (1981) and "spiritual pollution" (1983). Various "forbidden zones" (*jinqu*) have been opened one by one: romantic love, the violence of the Cultural Revolution, the problem of juvenile delinquency, and many others. Some topics, such as the personal responsibility of Mao for the Cultural Revolution, have been only partially opened; that is, they have been made safe for veiled expression only.

In broad terms, two of the major areas most affected by the relaxation of control have been traditional Chinese culture and Western culture. In sheer volume, nothing compares with the reemergence of traditional arts such as local opera, storytelling, comedians' dialogues, and other popular performing arts, especially in the countryside. Western observers—almost entirely lacking access to rural and popular culture; interested as we are in questions relating to Western influences, artistic caliber, and political controls; and further reinforced in these interests because our Chinese intellectual friends share them—can easily overlook the important fact that, for the majority of Chinese, the relaxation has meant simply that one can enjoy again what one always used to enjoy. Villains and heroes like Cao Cao and Liu Bang, as well as fox fairies and the ghosts of monks, are once again welcome on the opera stage. Modern themes are making inroads, to be sure—especially in the supremely popular comedians' dialogues. But a glance at the show announcements in most city newspapers will show that traditional performances easily outnumber modern ones. In rural areas, this is even more the case.

Western cultural imports, while not as great in volume as the resurgence of traditional arts, have come more quickly and in greater quantity than at any other time in the history of the People's Republic. By 1984, thousands of European and American literary works were being translated and published annually, in literally hundreds of periodicals. Yet most of these circulated only in the thousands and among the elite. At a more popular level, Western films and television productions have been made available to millions and have sometimes led to major fads. The French-Italian film *Zorro* was immensely popular in China's principal cities in the early 1980s. The American television series "Man from Atlantis" was shown nationally in one-hour episodes on Saturday evenings in 1979-1980, to a much larger audience than it had, or could ever have had, in the West.

On the whole, the selection of Western books, films, and television programs for introduction to China has been less than ideal. Aside from the necessary political screening, cost has been an important factor in the choice of films to be shown in China. The mediocre American movie *Convoy*, widely shown in 1979, was chosen by China because of its low price tag. The quality of the translations of literary works has been uneven. Yet another problem is an undeveloped sense of the distinction between best-sellers and "serious" works in the West. A translation of Herman Wouk's *Winds of War* has been widely read in China and is widely regarded as a modern American classic.

Serious Chinese writers in the post-Mao years, both inside and outside the party,[15] have obviously welcomed the wider scope for creativity allowed to them and to their readers. The reintroduction of Western literature has sparked interest in modernist techniques as well as the hope of raising artistic standards in contemporary Chinese writing. Gradually, stories[16] and poems[17] have appeared that not only have technical grace and subtlety but also treat universal human themes that can appeal to readers anywhere.

Much more common, however, are works that continue to show an "obsession with China," written by writers whose deepest worries are about the moral and spiritual well-being of China. For these writers and their readers, the relaxation of control has permitted the publication of more literary works that "tell the truth" about social and political problems in China, and this truth-telling has remained a cardinal literary virtue.[18] Yet the continuing strong interest in political and social commentary has produced certain ironies as the scope for literary expression has expanded. The basic motive for seeking more leeway has always been to open new areas for literary treatment serving both the pure artist in search of inspiration and the social critic in search of evidence. Ironically, however, the expansion of the scope of literary expression itself has become a preoccupying issue. Stories and poems have been written for little reason other than to test, or to challenge, the borderlines of permissibility. Thus, while the goal has been greater breadth, the result often has been another kind of narrowness. Politically charged works may require more daring, but truly good works are more difficult to write. When cultural policy has been most relaxed—as it was, for example, in the winter and spring of 1985—writers ironically have felt a new kind of pressure. In the words of Feng Mu, chief editor of the authoritative *Literary Gazette*, "if writers cannot produce good works under these conditions, they will have no excuses."[19] By contrast, when political pressures are strong, as they were in the fall of 1983, even a studied silence can seem eloquent.

Diffuseness and Volatility in Cultural Policy

As other chapters in this book make clear, many aspects of Chinese life can profitably be approached by analyzing top-level policy. Although subject to change over time and to variation in application, top-level policy exerts a sufficiently powerful and widespread influence to tell us much about what is going on. This is also true for cultural policy, but perhaps a bit less so than for certain other fields. In looking at cultural policy as well, it is crucial to bear in mind that influence originates from several sources, and that there is a complex fluidity, even volatility, in policy.

An underlying cause of this diffuseness and fluidity of policy is that literature continues to be widely regarded as a vehicle for important, if sometimes subtle, political expression. The first signs of major upheavals, such as the Cultural Revolution, appeared in literature and "literary" criticism. Hence, almost everyone in China, whatever his or her specialty, is well advised to maintain a side interest in literature. Whether one uses literature to advance one's own views, or merely to monitor the direction in which things are going, literature remains important. Even the People's Liberation Army employs literary critics, such as Liu Baiyu and Huang Gang, who watch cultural developments and sometimes play very active roles in them. (The contrast with American society is stunning, of course. Can we imagine distress in the Pentagon about Kurt Vonnegut's latest novel?)

Another underlying cause of the diffuseness and fluidity in cultural policy is the relative ease with which it can be reversed. Dwight Perkins points out in Chapter 2 that post-Mao economic reforms, which allow a larger proportion of China's national product to go to personal consumption, could be reversed only at the risk of widespread riots. But literature is far more changeable. One can launch a gambit in literary form (only to withdraw it if necessary) and produce a great deal of talk and worry, but no riots. This is basically what happened, at the national level, in the leftist-sponsored "spiritual pollution" campaign that came and went so abruptly in the fall and winter of 1983-1984. Similar events constantly occur on a smaller scale and in limited areas. The reversibility of cultural trends also helps to explain why literature is often the first area in which dissenting views are aired. It is easier to write a story protesting the system of work assignments than actually to protest the system of work assignments.

What causes cultural policy to change? Broadly speaking, there are two kinds of reasons for such change: (1) shifts in the power relations among groups or factions with different views; and (2) ambivalence, and thus occasional changes, in the feelings of key individuals in the cultural field.

Writers who have trouble publishing their work, or difficulty in defending themselves once it is published, often seek support from more powerful persons or groups. The supporting party is called the writer's "backstage" (*houtai*). Typically a high official (someone in a key position—sometimes a publisher or editor), a backstage supporter may be interested in serving as *houtai* because a writer can publish a viewpoint that the official approves but would find "inconvenient" to express publicly himself. Sometimes a backstage supporter will give broad support to whatever a writer, or group of writers, might say in general, with no commitment to support any one statement in particular. The support of a writer can, in other words, vary in specificity as well as in strength. In nearly all cases there remains at least some ambiguity in the relationship between supporter and writer, because the supporter prefers not to become too concretely accountable for what the writer says. (The tie between the two is least ambiguous when it is cemented by extraliterary factors such as blood relationships. An extreme—and therefore perfectly clear—case is the tie between Ye Xiangzhen, director of the 1981 film "Wilderness," and her father, Marshall Ye Jianying. The fact that this film could stretch the limits of permissibility in its romantic dialogue and scenery is certainly attributable to the director's connection with Marshall Ye, although clearly not to his own artistic views.)

Alliances among writers and supporters can shift, depending on the time, place, and issue. When controversies arise, writers and editors on two sides of a question may look for support wherever they can find it, and the decision as to whether a work can be published or not, or whether a writer will be criticized or not, depends on which side carries more weight, politically, at the crucial moment. Regional variations are important in these balances. In 1980 everyone knew, for example, that the literary authorities in Anhui were much more permissive than those in Hebei, where conservatism was championed. Guangdong was also known to be permissive but was more famous for openness about love and sex, whereas the literary authorities in Anhui were more willing to allow the exposure of social and political problems. The literary magazines in Peking were also relatively permissive in the late 1970s, but when a Guangdong literary magazine boldly attacked Hao Ran for his part in the Cultural Revolution, they sided with Hao Ran (China's foremost novelist during that period) and his local supporters in Peking.

In other words, a balance can sometimes tip one way in one place and another way somewhere else. Writers, aware of the differing views of key individuals in different locales, began in the post-Mao period to submit their manuscripts according to editorial bent, even if it meant mailing them the length and breadth of China. Thus, the regional differences in the publishing scene gave increased flexibility to writers. The more liberal-minded editors, for their part, began to monitor one another informally so as to advance or retreat in concert and thereby to avoid someone's publishing an extreme view that might be singled out for attack by doctrinaire opponents.

The fluidity just described depends upon the interactions among individuals. However, individuals are not fixed in their own orientations; changes in individual views, both large and small, further complicate the shifts of policy. Some of these changes are brought on by social pressures. The young writer Li Jian, for example, publicly championed a Maoist view in the spring of 1979, was severely criticized as a result, and decided to renounce those views. By 1981 and 1982, he had gone to the opposite extreme of writing lurid tales of social corruption.[20] Other writers, succumbing to different pressures, have apparently switched from liberalism to a kind of pseudoleftism designed to please their superiors.[21]

Ultimately, however, changes of views rooted in genuine ambivalence about what is best for China are more important than those that result from external pressures. The senior poet Ai Qing, expressing his resentment toward heavy-handed political critics of literature that attempts to tell the truth, wrote in 1980:

> If you are ugly
> Don't blame the mirror.

And:

> Only an idiot
> Argues with an idiot.[22]

Yet, hardly three years later, Ai Qing was siding with the doctrinaire critics in charging young writers with "spiritual pollution." Why? The suggestion that Ai Qing is simply an addled old man, as some have charged, is not plausible; nor should one conclude that such an intrepid veteran caved in to political pressure. Ai Qing's shift in attitude bespeaks a profound ambivalence over the most central question in Chinese intellectual history of the last hundred years: How and how much should China change (and with what sacrifice of "Chineseness") in order to accommodate technical modernization and the cultural trappings of the West that inevitably accompany it? In 1980, Ai Qing was opposing the xenophobia and fatuous pride of Maoism in its final phase; in 1983, on the other horn of the great dilemma, he was indignant about the silly aping of foreign ways by youth. His views are not "mind changes" so much as expressions of two sides of a profound and difficult ambivalence.

Although impossible to prove, it seems likely that sudden shifts in cultural policy can occur because a top leader, such as Deng Xiaoping, undergoes a private, and perhaps quite subtle, shift of views. Without this assumption, it is difficult to explain how a minority view, such as the one favoring the campaign to "oppose spiritual pollution,"[23] could so suddenly become dominant, as it did in October 1983, and then, so shortly thereafter, in February 1984, fall out of favor. The fact that delicate balances in the minds of a few top leaders, or even a single leader, can result in such major policy swings is yet another reason why cultural policy is so volatile.

Modernist Trends

It is sometimes observed that the process called "modernization" exerts homogenizing pressures on every society it touches. Although societies naturally vary in the speeds and forms of their modernization, tendencies toward specialization of work, routinization of life, and the emergence of "universalistic" interpersonal relations do seem universal and perhaps inevitable.[24] Resistance to these tendencies is often strongest in the cultural sphere or, more precisely, in those aspects of culture that most profoundly define a national tradition. This is certainly true of China. China's writers, as I have argued earlier, are still strongly conditioned by traditional conceptions of a writer's proper role; on the other hand, the allure of "modernism" is growing, especially among young writers and readers. The collision between these two tendencies has many aspects, of which two are particularly worth noting.

First, modernization imposes increased specialization upon intellectuals, who do not necessarily welcome it. True, scientific intellectuals in post-Mao China have accepted the necessity for specialization quite well. Some of those sent to the West for advanced training have even honed their skills beyond a level that can easily be used in China. But many literary intellectuals have clung to the ideal of the generalist, of the broadly relevant person. They do not seek narrow expertise so much as learning and self-cultivation so whole and well-integrated as to be coextensive with morality itself. Demands for specialization of role, or "field," which issue all too often from the "scientific" socialist bureaucracy, can run against their grain. As just one example of the problem, the major publishing houses in China assign editors to review fiction manuscripts according to what province, or county, a manuscript is submitted from. Editor A reads the Hebei manuscripts, editor B the Shandong manuscripts, and so on. Such arbitrary "specialization" seems counterintuitive to people who still implicitly assume a duty to "take responsibility for the world."

Second, as mentioned earlier, Chinese intellectuals have traditionally felt that morality and power begin within and radiate outward—from self to family to the world. In contrast, the history of modernist literature is one of exploration within, into the psyche, into "preformal" use of language, and so on. This peering inward appears to be a consequence of the general process of modernization. Human beings in modern cities, as Georg Simmel has argued, ironically come to feel isolated inside their new environments; human contacts, while extensive, become drained of emotion or commitment. Readers and writers of modern fiction, sharing a need to escape isolation, find nowhere to reach but within. The modern novel developed as an answer to their needs.[25] To the extent that Simmel's analysis is correct, it seems likely that China will produce more inward-looking literature as it continues to modernize. However, such literature runs counter to China's tradition of outward-looking, socially committed literature, based on Confucianism and reinforced in the "May Fourth" period of the 1920s and early 1930s, which is still by far the dominant approach in Chinese letters.

The post-Mao period has already witnessed some interesting experiments in modernist literary techniques, although it is hard to say to what extent these are consequences of modernization in Simmel's sense or simply the result of conscious imitation of Western examples. For a few years, from about 1978 to 1981, "stream-of-consciousness" writing was popular among university students of literature. A few stories by the established writer Wang Meng were held up as models of this technique,[26] although none of his works came as close to the writings of James Joyce as some of the creative mash published informally by youth.[27] In poetry, it has been the young writers of "murky poetry" (*menglong shi*) who have led the way in modernism. An example is "Feeling" by Gu Cheng:

> The sky is gray
> The road is gray
> The building is gray
> The rain is gray
>
> In this blanket of dead gray
> Two children walk by,
> One bright red
> One pale green.[28]

Both stream-of-consciousness fiction and "murky poetry" have met some strong opposition. Two kinds of complaints, which might be called "artistic" and "political," have been lodged against them. The artistic criticisms have come from well-established poets such as Ai Qing and Gu Gong (father of Gu Cheng, the young poet just quoted), who complain that if a poet has something to say, then he or she ought simply to say it. They find "murky poetry" lacking patriotism, concern for the poor, opposition to injustice, and other heartfelt values that have given their own poetry its power. Why write something that cannot move readers because readers cannot even understand it? What good will that do?

The basis for "political" criticisms has been the feeling that if writers fail to spell out what they mean, an open question remains as to what in fact they do mean and what, in the end, they have communicated. Of course, one can never be certain of exactly what a reader derives from any literary work, even a very realistic one. But, in "murky poetry," what does it imply to say that everything is "gray"? Or worse, "dead" gray? What can it mean to describe children as red and green? The problem is not only that subversive interpretations are possible; even if none were intended by the author or perceived by the reader, the implicit claim of the "murky" poet is that there is a legitimate sphere of literary life within which the clumsy categories of political criticism ("correct" and "incorrect") simply do not apply. The poet makes, in a sense, a declaration of artistic autonomy within the literary sphere, and it implies that political controls, which had always limited creativity, themselves are subject to limits.

Lack of Overt Dissidence

With the beginnings of the cultural thaw in China after Mao, Westerners were eager to find signs of "literary dissidence" of the kind we are accustomed to seeing in the Soviet Union. The unofficial Chinese journals that appeared, both political and literary, were somewhat hastily called *samizdat* (literally, "self-published") journals, like their Soviet counterparts. But the resemblance to the Soviet case is only partial. Soviet "dissidents," beleaguered though they may be, are much better established inside the Soviet Union, and much better recognized outside of the country, than their counterparts in China. The Soviet "underground" press is apparently strong enough that it cannot be stamped out; major dissidents enjoy reputations in the West, and sometimes derive protection from this fact. Leading dissident works, such as those of Boris Pasternak and Aleksandr Solzhenitsyn, while unpublishable in the Soviet Union, are widely published and admired in the West. But this is not the case in China. Even Soviet "in-house" dissidents, such as Ilia Ehrenberg and Yevgeny Yevtuchenko, have expressed themselves more bluntly and openly than has any Chinese literary figure.

The reasons for these differences between the two giant Communist states are more complex than one might assume. Three factors may help to explain them.

First, the literary control systems are different. The Soviet Union's is more explicit and mechanical, while China's is more subtle and psychological. The Soviet Union has a censorship organ called the Chief Administration for the Preservation of State Secrets in the Press, or *Glavlit* for short. This great bureaucracy of 70,000 or more persons reviews all galley proofs in a systematic way. It also publishes and updates a large handbook for its personnel, telling just what points and phrases are out of bounds. China, in contrast, has no such bureaucracy or handbook. Control is exercised through authoritative warnings from top leaders against, for example, "bourgois liberalism" or "spiritual pollution." It is the responsibility of each publisher, editor, and writer to interpret the vague phrases in such warnings and to judge how much can be risked in concrete cases. As noted earlier, the willingness to take risks depends on one's own status, on the power of one's supporters, and even on one's geographical location— as well, of course, as on one's personal courage or foolhardiness.

In China, moreover, the punishment for going too far can be reprimand by one's superiors or, for nationally significant cases, criticism in the public press. Reprimand and criticism are not merely a matter of "losing face"; typically the reprimanding superior also has the power to determine a person's salary, housing, medical care, children's education, permission to travel, access to rationed commodities, and more. In addition, for writers there is a lingering uncertainty over whether the truly brutal methods of the Cultural Revolution are really gone forever. Even a conscious belief that they are does not eradicate emotional associations with the word *criticism.*

In short, the Chinese control system, while much more subtle, diffuse, and psychological—and therefore superficially more gentle in appearance—is nonetheless more penetrating and pervasive than the Soviet system, and often it is more effectively intimidating as well. Ironically, the long list of rules in the Soviets' *Glavlit* handbook can have a liberating effect in comparison with the Chinese controls. Although Chinese writers must always make private estimates of what is riskable, and may worry even when they need not, their Soviet counterparts apparently can be somewhat more relaxed about expressing themselves so long as they stay within the formal rules of *Glavlit.*

Second, a Chinese writer, because of the traditional conception of what an intellectual should be, finds even the appearance of disloyalty to China (and its policy) a very difficult option. Bai Hua, who has suffered more public criticism than any other writer in post-Mao China, told the Convention of the All-China Writers' Association in December 1984 that "a true Chinese writer must be, first and foremost, a true son of China."[29] A writer's duty to China has little to do with whether China is strong or weak, rich or poor, or whether its government is harsh or gentle. The duty exists because China is China, still and always the basic fact in the Chinese universe. A writer should speak on behalf of China and its people—courageously if necessary. If his or her views are accepted by political leaders, fine; if they are not, the writer does not hawk them elsewhere but withdraws to await a more propitious time.

To a Chinese writer, the Soviet dissident's alternative of publishing "underground," or in the West, runs counter to some deeply embedded Chinese notions of the duties of the intellectual. (The Chinese writers who published in the "unofficial journals" during the period 1978–1980 clearly did so less from preference than from lack of access to the official media.) Soviet and Chinese political leaders have also differed in their assumptions about their roles in ensuring the unity of the nation's literature and politics. Khrushchev, in the wake of Stalin, repeatedly insisted that he was no literary critic and did not want to tell writers how to write (even though he did, occasionally). By contrast, Hu Yaobang finds it not at all out of place to deliver authoritative statements at major literary meetings. And most Chinese writers accept this as quite natural. They assume that writers are, or should be, tied to the national polity.

Third, Soviet literary dissidence thrives in part because of the moral and political support coming from the West. A reputation in the West, if it is large enough to make a person newsworthy, can afford a certain protection to a Soviet dissident. No such reputations have yet developed for Chinese writers, except, to some degree, within the Overseas Chinese community. There appear to be several reasons for this particular contrast between China and the Soviet Union. No major Chinese writer is as explicitly dissident as some of those in the Soviet Union; thus a Westerner has to read more subtly to find dissent. The Russian literary tradition, moreover, is closer to Western tradition than that of China; thus Western intellectuals naturally find Soviet writers more interesting and congenial from a literary point of view. In addition, cold war issues between the West and the Soviet Union have heightened the Western zest for uncovering the "dark side" of the adversary. (China, by comparison, can be very harsh indeed before losing its charm for Western intellectuals.) More concretely, the issue of emigration of Jewish intellectuals from the Soviet Union touches Westerners personally in ways that the plight of Chinese writers has not so far—except, again, in some Overseas Chinese circles. But whatever the causes of the phenomenon may be, it certainly exists: A would-be Chinese dissident cannot expect much effective support from the West.

Writers' Livelihood

Generally speaking, the biggest worries of writers in post-Mao China have been those over issues relating to art, society, and politics—not personal finances. (This generalization may be less true for many younger and less established writers.) Nonetheless, problems of livelihood have generated some irritation, and even bitterness.

Chinese writers currently can be paid for their work in one of three or four ways.[30] A small minority have "professional" status, meaning that their work unit is formally the Writers' Association, which pays them a monthly salary that is basically equivalent to what they would earn if they worked for a school or factory. The benefits of being a "professional" writer include prestige and more time for writing, but seldom more salary. (In the early 1980s, professional writers were paid 70 to 100 or more yuan per month, and in rare cases as much as 300 yuan.)[31] In addition to receiving a salary, any writer, whether amateur or professional, is given a "manuscript payment" of about 7 to 10 yuan per thousand characters when a manuscript is accepted for publication. (In the case of poetry, twenty lines, regardless of length, count as a thousand characters.) If the manuscript is a book, the writer receives, in addition to the manuscript payment, "print-run payments," calculated at 3 percent of the manuscript payment for each 10,000 copies printed. If a work is made into a film, the author gets a one-time payment from 1,000 to 1,500 yuan. But even these payments combined seldom amount to much. Zhang Yang's novel, *The Second Handshake*, which has been the most lucrative work by a post-Mao author, brought the author a total of probably 6,000 yuan at most. Published short stories, even ones by famous writers, normally bring less than 100 yuan, and most novels less than 500.

Yet, in the early 1980s, writers were much better paid than they had been in the early 1970s, when the only material rewards for a published manuscript were typically gifts—a few books or maybe a pen. The discontent that has arisen in the post-Mao years results from comparisons not with the past but with others in society who are now doing better, or are perceived to be doing better, under the new reforms. Explicitly socialist as they may be, many Chinese writers find it difficult to accept the fact that some peasants might be earning tens of thousands of yuan when they, as intellectuals, cannot. The bonuses given to factory workers, while relatively small, also seem unfairly easy to get compared with the hard-earned payment received for a published short story. An irreverent ditty that circulated informally in the early 1980s satirized the "Four Modernizations" (*sihua*) as "Peasants are free-marketized (*ziyouhua*), workers are bonusized (*jiangjinhua*), cadres are back-doorized (*houmenhua*), and intellectuals are impoverished (*pinkunhua*)." Its message pertains to teachers and intellectuals generally, not just to writers.

Writers complain of certain specific obstacles to fair remuneration for them. Since China has no copyright law, their works are often reprinted without permission and without payment of fees. Even when publishers do pay, the question of which manuscripts they take, and how large to make the print runs, are determined by the publisher's own calculations, into which politics, both national and personal, figure importantly. In the mid-1980s, a new irritation arose. China's serious writers began to feel sharp resentment toward the large-scale publication of popular fiction, such as reprintings of *The Adventures of Sherlock Holmes*. Such printings could lead to big profits for publishers, themselves now working under the economic "responsibility system," but they produced no payments for authors.

Money is only part of the question of "livelihood," however. Many important questions of welfare—housing, medical care, education for one's children—and even such relatively minor matters as whether one can ride first or second class on the railroad, or has access to good theater tickets and good restaurants, are determined primarily not by money but by one's official status or unofficial connections. Zhang Jie, one of the best known and most loved writers of the post-Mao period, still lives in a dormitory in a machinery institute where she worked as an accountant in the mid-1970s. She shares her tiny quarters with her mother and (until 1984) her daughter. There can be no question that Zhang Jie's many published stories and books have brought her enough money to pay the marginally higher rent that housing would cost. The problem is obtaining permission. Spaces are few, and demand is strong. A national literary reputation does not necessarily translate into clout with the key people who make housing allocations. Chen Jiangong, a young writer of considerable reputation, had to spend nearly a year in 1983-1984 doing what is popularly called *pao fangzi,* or "running after housing"—that is, running around bestowing the gifts and obeisances necessary to get housing.

Thus even housing and other benefits can depend upon political questions and "backstage" support. When a writer calculates the size and nature of the literary risks he or she might take, personal material factors sometimes have to be considered.

The Future

Changes in cultural policy in China are often not easy to explain, even after decades have passed. Just why cultural policy was dramatically relaxed in 1956, only to be followed by a crackdown in 1957, is still unclear; the issue is still a matter of debate among intellectuals both inside China and outside. When the past is so problematic, one analyzes the future with trepidation; but perhaps a few observations can be hazarded about the next decade or so.

The centuries-old assumptions about the role of intellectuals, briefly sketched above, cannot disappear overnight. Many writers will remain "obsessed with China," and will continue to see their efforts to "tell the truth" about social or political conditions and to "speak for the people" as exalted duties—and as *literary* values. These values will persist, as they have in the past, through political campaigns that temporarily prevent their overt expression. At the same time, as long as modernization continues, the influence of literary modernism will increase. It is a reasonable hope that some writers, especially among the younger generation, will produce works of high quality as measured by international standards for modern literature.

The limitations laid down by political authorities on the scope of the freedom available to writers are unlikely to disappear. Even at its widest, this scope has always had limits. In recent years, its outer limits have been defined by four principles requiring continuation of the leadership of the party, the socialist system, the dictatorship of the proletariat, and correct Marxism-Leninism. Although the catchwords may change in the future, the principle that allows the party to circumscribe writers is not likely to meet serious challenge. Some writers will continue to be irritated as long as *any* limits on scope are imposed. But for most, who accept the fact of limits, the big question is *how wide* the scope will be. There is a tremendous practical difference, for instance, between the atmosphere of December 1984, when Hu Qili, speaking for the top leadership, called for "freedom of creativity," and that of November 1983, when austere warnings about "spiritual pollution" stifled all interesting expression except the subtle question of who could maintain the most meaningful silence. There is still the possibility that policy will swerve, or even lurch, again. A lurching can happen even while policies in economic and other spheres remain more stable. In the generally good literary weather of 1985, it is hard to imagine an abrupt reversal. But, then, the crackdown of autumn 1983 would have been hard to imagine in early 1983.

Two important factors weigh against a return to tight controls on culture over a decade or more: First, Party Chairman Hu Yaobang seems, from almost all available evidence, to involve himself personally in cultural policy and to side with those who favor relaxation of controls. The younger leaders being recruited in China's cultural bureaucracy also seem to be basically in Hu's camp. Second, the geographical and political diffuseness of the literary scene, as described earlier, will continue to give a certain flexibility to writers, even if top-level policy tightens. This is not to say that a totalitarian cultural policy could never be reimposed, but only that it would be much more difficult now than before the Cultural Revolution to bring it back.

Notes

1. Huang Ruixu, "Investigation of Current Trends Among Young Workers Concerning Appreciation of Literature and Art: A Survey of Tianjin, Shanghai, Wuhan, Guangzhou, Shenyang, Lanzhou, Beijing, and Shenzhen," *Dangdai wenyi shichao* (Lanzhou), no. 4 (1984), pp. 49–63. Reprinted in Joint Publications Research Service (JPRS), November 20, 1984, pp. 41–61.

2. *Daxue* [The Great Learning], ch. 1 in *Sishu baihua jujie* [Vernacular Commentary on the Confucian Four Books] (Hong Kong: Cultural Library Company, 1968), p. 12.

3. "He who excels at ruling is a learner; he who excels at learning is a ruler." See *Analects of Confucius,* Zizhang chapter; *Sishu baihua jujie,* p. 155.

4. Fan Zhongyan, "Qiuyanglouji," in *Guwen guanzhi,* vol. 9 (Hong Kong: Xuelin Bookstore, n.d.), p. 138.

5. C. T. Hsia, *A History of Modern Chinese Fiction* (New Haven, Conn.: Yale University Press, 1971), pp. 533–554.

6. Lu Xun, "Preface," in *Nahan* [Outcry] (Hong Kong: Huitong Bookstore, 1972), pp. 3–5.

7. The epithet was originally taken from a particular story called "Scar" (*Shanghen*), by Lu Xinhua, published in *Wenhuibao* (Shanghai), August 11, 1978. The story was translated as "The Wounded" in Geremie Barme and Bennett Lee (eds.), *The Wounded* (Hong Kong: Joint Publishing Company, 1979).

8. Examples are "Ren yao zhijian" (*People's Literature,* vol. 9 [1979], pp. 83–102) and other works by Liu Binyan. See Perry Link (ed.), *"People or Monsters?" and Other Stories and Reportage from China After Mao* (Bloomington: Indiana University Press, 1983).

9. The concern of scientists for literary toleration can be seen, for example, in Xu Liangying and Fan Dainian, *Science and Socialist Construction in China* (Armonk, N.Y.: M. E. Sharpe, 1982), ch. 5.

10. *Guangming Daily,* September 26, 1981.

11. In certain cases, the mutual loyalty of a writer and a leader is clear enough that, with reasonable confidence, one can infer a leader's attitude from a writer's expression. On the present point, the writings of Liu Binyan can be assumed to be reasonably close to the views of Hu Yaobang.

12. Liu Binyan, "Listen Carefully to the Voice of the People" (speech at the Fourth Congress of Chinese Literature and Art Workers, Peking, November 9, 1979), translated in Link, *People or Monsters?* pp. 3–4.

13. See Hu Qili's speech at the Fourth Congress of the Writers' Association, *People's Daily,* December 30, 1984, p. 1.

14. Wang Zhongcai, "Desert Scenes," *Shikan* 10 (1979), translated in Perry Link (ed.), *Stubborn Weeds: Popular and Controversial Chinese Literature After the Cultural Revolution* (Bloomington: Indiana University Press, 1983), p. 189. Reprinted by permission.

15. It is a mistake to suppose that party members generally favor control of writers whereas nonparty writers press for free expression. Writers such as Bai Hua and Liu Binyan, who have been most outspoken in the cause of writers' freedom and most widely criticized for being so, are party members.

16. See Michael S. Duke (ed.), *Contemporary Chinese Literature: An Anthology of Post-Mao Fiction and Poetry* (Armonk, N.Y.: M. E. Sharpe, 1985).

17. See William Tay, "Obscure Poetry," in Jeffrey Kinkley (ed.), *After Mao* (Cambridge, Mass.: Harvard University Press, 1985).

18. It is important to stress that truth-telling is considered a *literary* virtue. Works that "tell the truth about China" are sometimes viewed in the West as, *ipso facto,* "less artistic" than those that treat universal human questions. But this view can be misleading. There are, first of all, important artistic gradations among works by writers who are preoccupied with China. Moreover,

the power of the better works in this category to move readers is greatest among those readers who, like the authors, feel it the proper calling of literature to be preoccupied with social and political questions.

19. Feng Mu, conversation with the author, Los Angeles, April 11, 1985.

20. See Kam Louie, "Between Paradise and Hell: Literary Double-Think in Post-Mao China," *Australian Journal of Chinese Affairs*, no. 10 (July 1983), pp. 1–15.

21. Without naming names, Wang Meng, chief editor of *People's Literature*, reports this tendency in "The Golden Age of Socialist Literature Has Arrived," *People's Daily*, January 6, 1985, p. 3.

22. Ai Qing, "Roses and Thorns," *People's Daily*, July 10, 1980, translated in Perry Link, ed., *Roses and Thorns: The Second Blooming of the Hundred Flowers in Chinese Fiction, 1979–80* (Berkeley and Los Angeles: University of California Press, 1984), pp. v–vi. Reprinted by permission.

23. Ai Qing, *People's Daily*, November 2, 1983, p. 3.

24. The argument that modernization is a "universal social solvent" is made, in a shrewd albeit flamboyant fashion, by Marion J. Levy, Jr., in *Modernization: Latecomers and Survivors* (New York: Basic Books, 1972).

25. Georg Simmel, "The Metropolis and Mental Life," in Paul K. Hatt and Albert J. Reiss, Jr. (eds.), *Reader in Urban Sociology* (Glencoe, Ill., 1951), pp. 563–574.

26. See, for example, "Eye of the Night" (*Ye de yan*), "Voices of Spring" (*Chun zhi sheng*), and other stories collected in *The Butterfly and Other Stories* (Peking: Panda Books, 1983).

27. See, for example, An Dong, "The Sea Does Not Belong to Us," *Zheiyidai*, no. 1, translated by Dale R. Johnson in Link, *Stubborn Weeds*, pp. 170–179.

28. Gu Cheng, "Feeling," *Shikan* 10 (1980), translated by William Tay in Link, *Stubborn Weeds*, p. 185. Reprinted by permission.

29. *People's Daily*, December 31, 1984, p. 7.

30. For a fuller discussion of writers' pay, see the introduction to Ai Qing, *Roses and Thorns*, pp. 25–29.

31. One yuan is currently worth about US$ .50; in 1980, it was worth about $ .66.

5
Social Trends in China: The Triumph of Inequality?

Martin King Whyte

Major changes have occurred in China since the death of Mao Zedong, yet questions remain about how to interpret those changes. Some see China retreating from utopianism and returning to rationality. Others see a triumph of the counter-revolution that Mao had long feared and the demise of his "revolutionary immortality."

Another popular interpretation of the changes that have taken place—perhaps the most widely accepted interpretation—is one emphasizing Mao's dissatisfaction, in his later years, with the social consequences of economic development. He saw that development threatening the egalitarian goals of the revolution. The Great Leap Forward of 1958, and then the Cultural Revolution of 1966, according to this interpretation, were motivated by Mao's effort to subordinate economic development to those egalitarian goals. For example, one commentator recently argued that during the Cultural Revolution the radicals in China were "trying to remold China in their utopian image of an egalitarian, non-bureaucratic, ideologically motivated, and self-reliant society."[1] If, in the process, economic development was slowed or even stalled, that was a necessary price to pay for the preservation and enhancement of social equality. According to this argument, Mao's successors, and perhaps Deng Xiaoping in particular, also perceive a basic conflict between economic development and social equality, at least in the short run, but their solution is the opposite of Mao's. In response to the economic dislocations and stagnation of the late Mao years (which, as Dwight Perkins notes in Chapter 2, the Deng leadership often exaggerates), what China needs is economic development full speed ahead. If, to achieve this end, more inequality must be tolerated in order to speed up the economy, then so be it; let the egalitarian goals of the revolution be sacrificed. Hence, in Deng's view, as well as in Mao's, equality and economic development are in conflict, but now economic development has won out.

This popular argument is at best misleading and at worst simply wrong. Realities in China often do not match official rhetoric. Moreover, an oversimplified view of how to conceptualize and measure inequality has caused much confusion. It will be argued here that China, in Mao's final years, was not a very egalitarian place and that China today may not be moving full speed ahead in promoting inequality. However, there is a rather serious obstacle to presenting this revisionist view convincingly. In spite of the increasing streams of information being released in recent years in the People's Republic of China, there is still little systematically organized data available that would enable one to judge whether various kinds of inequality actually are increasing or decreasing. So, for the moment, with the required evidence not in hand, we must rely on scraps of evidence and logic to support the position that the concept of "Maoist egalitarians versus Dengist inegalitarians" is misguided.[2]

The Rhetoric of Equality and Inequality

The idea that during the Maoist era, and during the Cultural Revolution decade in particular, there was a broad-ranging egalitarian push, and that the current leaders in China almost delight in repudiating egalitarianism and singing the praises of inequality, is not simply a mirage. To understand realities, we must examine in detail the policies and rhetoric that have characterized both eras.

Mao's antipathy toward the emerging stratification of the new China he led was already visible in the late 1950s, and a variety of measures were taken in the 1960s and 1970s—right up until his death in 1976—that seemed designed to check inequalities of various kinds. The Soviet-style development of the 1950s was seen as disproportionately benefiting urbanites and increasing rural-urban inequality. In the early 1960s, slogans such as "Agriculture First" and "Industry Should Serve Agriculture" were promoted; moreover, China initiated its own version of the "green revolution" and raised procurement prices while lowering the prices of some manufactured goods, thereby improving the terms of trade for the peasants. Periodically, large numbers of urbanites were "sent down" to serve agriculture, and restrictions on migration kept talented rural youths from fleeing to the cities. The urban bias in the health field was attacked, and barefoot doctors and rural cooperative medical insurance systems were established to help meet village needs. Vigorous efforts were also made to open more rural schools and expand their enrollments. Urban wage levels were for the most part frozen after 1963, whereas rural incomes were still allowed to grow. Measures such as these convinced many observers that the rural-urban gap was being reduced in Mao's China.[3]

In addition, Mao was becoming increasingly concerned about the status and privileges of intellectuals. Many of the financial benefits available to intellectuals, such as royalty payments and prizes for innovations, were eliminated during the Cultural Revolution. The arrogance of intellectuals was supposed to have been countered by periodic spells of political study and manual labor, such as in the "May 7th Cadre Schools" (rural indoctrination centers for cadres and others) set up after 1968. Professional prerogatives were attacked, and during the Cultural Revolution senior intellectuals had to share the stage with peasant-teachers, amateur writers, and worker and soldier administrators. In some cases, actual status reversals were tried, as when doctors were required to empty bedpans while nurses tried their hand at surgery. The educational system was transformed in an effort to produce literate manual laborers rather than technical experts, and an attempt was made to take schools out of the business of identifying and developing talent to determine who would get ahead. In general, an anti-expertise ethos was stressed, and the argument was made that progress is determined mainly by the enthusiasm and vigorous labor of the workers, peasants, and soldiers, rather than by the knowledge of the experts.

Perhaps the main targets of Mao's antipathy were the cadres in positions of power in the party and in the state bureaucracy. They were seen as showing tendencies toward becoming a privileged group interested in promoting stratification. During the Cultural Revolution itself, large numbers of high-ranking cadres were purged. Those who remained in office or were later rehabilitated were also expected to cleanse themselves periodically with stints in the May 7th Cadre Schools. Special privileges for cadres in such areas as housing, dining halls, and schooling for their children were attacked, and those who engaged in "bourgeois" life-styles (for example, by playing bridge or tennis) were subjected to ridicule. Bureaucrats had to share power with workers, People's Liberation Army (PLA) soldiers, and mass representatives in "revolutionary committees," which represented a new form of administration.

All such policies were accompanied by egalitarian rhetoric. Piece rates, bonuses, and other material incentives to motivate work efforts were denounced as "sugar-coated bullets of the bourgeoisie," and they were largely eliminated. The graded wage system was seen as incorporating "bourgeois right," and Mao and his radical colleagues toyed with the idea of abolishing even this differentiating device.[4] Ranks and uniforms that indicated grades were eliminated from the PLA in 1965. A standardized "proletarian" style of life and dress was enforced throughout the population. Customs and tendencies that contributed to social differentiation, from the raising of goldfish to the frequenting of teahouses, were discouraged or suppressed. In general, there was an effort during the Cultural Revolution decade to foster what Susan Shirk has called a "virtuocracy," in which, in theory, any individual could earn merit by showing the proper political consciousness and dedication; yet virtue was viewed as its own reward, without leading to important material benefits or perquisites.[5]

Since Mao's death and the rehabilitation and increasing dominance of Deng Xiaoping, most of these policies and slogans have been repudiated. Egalitarianism has been vigorously denounced, and the virtues as well as the necessity of material incentives have been lauded. Several wage increases have been implemented, and these increasingly have been based on expertise and contributions rather than on seniority or political virtue. Piece rates, bonuses, royalty payments, and other material incentive devices have been reestablished and are now proliferating. The school system has again become hierarchical and highly competitive; academic performance is stressed, and good exam grades will put one on the track to a promising career. The May 7th Cadre Schools have been closed, and manual labor assignments for intellectuals and cadres have been reduced to a minimum so that experts and bureaucrats can devote their full energies to their specialized tasks. The high status of doctors and other specialists is once again being emphasized, and most of the nurse-surgeons, peasant-teachers, and other beneficiaries of the earlier policies have been returned to their lower status. The PLA has restored official ranks and the accompanying rank insignia and uniforms. Specialists are being accorded a variety of privileges, including preferential access to new apartments and transfers for family members living elsewhere. The idea that there is the danger of a "new class" or privileged bureaucratic stratum emerging is dismissed; everyone is said to belong to the laboring class now. It goes without saying that the Maoist dictum concerning the constant recurrence of class struggles has been repudiated.

In the countryside, the collectivized system of farming, with its built-in redistributive mechanisms, has been abandoned; the peasant family is again the basic farming unit in most of rural China. Moreover, it would seem that the order of the day in the villages is competition to get rich. The official press constantly lauds "specialized households" and "10,000-yuan households" and describes in great detail the new levels of consumption they enjoy. Pictures of peasants purchasing television sets, cassette recorders, new houses, tractors, and, in some cases, even automobiles and light airplanes are being used to stimulate envy and emulation of these new rich peasants. To those who worry that such trends may be leading to polarization in the countryside, the authorities answer with the slogan that "It Is Good to Get Rich." They argue that some people have to get rich first so that the new wealth will eventually trickle down to others. In response to arguments that some checks should be placed on this new accumulation of wealth, the first party secretary of Guangdong Province argued, "The 10,000 yuan households are not really rich. They should become still richer."[6] In urban areas as well, styles of life and dress are becoming increasingly differentiated, with official encouragement, as the uniform proletarian style of the late-Mao era is denigrated. In cities, as in villages, conspicuous consumption is seen as a beneficial trend rather than as a political deviation. The underlying rationale is that competition and envy are not alien to socialism. As the first party secretary of Heilongjiang Province put it, "The rewards [to intellectuals] should be so handsome that some people would not only feel jealous, but would also jump up and say, 'How outrageous!'"[7]

In sum, on the surface, policy and rhetoric in the late Mao era seemed to be promoting equality, whereas life in China today seems to be moving in just the opposite direction.

A Sociological Detour

Before considering the objections to acceptance of this view, we must take a brief detour into sociology. More specifically, it is necessary that we discuss the sorts of complications sociologists see whenever they try to talk about equality and inequality or compare the amount of either in any two countries or time periods.

First, we must consider the question: Equality or inequality in regard to what? Many comparisons focus on one aspect of stratification—often one that can be readily measured, such as the distribution of income, or related concepts such as consumption, property, or wealth. Yet it is clear that many other scarce resources exist that may be equally or unequally distributed and, perhaps particularly in a state socialist society, cannot all be reduced to monetary terms. Some specialists have devised lists of eight or ten separate dimensions of inequality, but for present purposes we will consider only the three primary dimensions that were the focus of the work of Max Weber: economic position, political power, and social status. The point to stress is that the extent of, and trends in, inequality along one dimension may not correspond to conditions along other dimensions.

A second issue concerns the measurement of equality or inequality along any one dimension. In this connection, there are several problems that defy easy solution. For one thing, power and status cannot be measured precisely. Moreover, even for something that is measurable, such as income, there are various kinds of statistics that can be used—standard deviations, maximum-minimum ratios, quintile or decile ratios, Gini coefficients, and so forth.[8] If unlimited information were available, the best course in general would be to use measures that capture the experience of an entire population, such as the Gini coefficient, rather than measures that rely only on parts of that population, such as maximum-minimum ratios.[9] But this general principle leads to a further question: What is the population to be analyzed? Ideally, one might wish to measure equality or inequality within the entire population of a country, but often data are available only for smaller units; for example, income distribution data may exist for a community or factory but not for larger units. The point to be stressed here is that it is quite possible for inequality to be decreasing within some subpopulations while it is increasing nationwide, or vice versa. Accordingly, we cannot generalize, from data on a subpopulation, about trends in the country at large.

Finally, when we consider political power, which cannot readily be quantified, we must look at what might be called both horizontal and vertical dimensions. The horizontal dimension is the extent to which there is equality or inequality among individuals, with respect to their political rights and privileges vis-à-vis the state—rights of citizenship, legal status, political participation rights, and so forth. The vertical dimension concerns the extent to which members of the general population are subordinated and powerless vis-à-vis the state, or have a high level of autonomy or influence in relation to the ruling authorities. Again, as power relations may become more equal along one dimension while becoming less equal along the other, we need to be quite clear about what sort of equality we are talking about.

One final complication completes this quick summary of stratification concepts. So far, the subject under discussion has been a static one, given the assumption that the stratification order and position of individuals within it remain fixed. But this is clearly not the case; on the contrary, we must consider whether there is equality or inequality in opportunities to move up or down in the stratification system, both within an individual's life span and from one generation to the next. The ideal comparison of equality and inequality, then, should take into account the wide range of vexing complications discussed here. Both the absence of data and space limitations prevent the inclusion of such an analysis here. In the pages that follow, however, attention will be focused on late-Mao and post-Mao trends regarding economic position and political power, although even in these two realms conclusions must remain tentative.[10]

The Realities of Stratification in the Late-Mao Era

The first trend to be noted is that, rhetoric aside, the late-Mao period was not one in which a systematic reduction of inequalities occurred; on the contrary, in many areas inequalities were increasing, owing, at least in part, to official policies. Let us first consider the economic situation and what we know about income distribution trends. The Marxist framework accepted by the Chinese Communist Party (CCP) sensitized Mao and other leaders to certain dimensions of inequality but blinded them to others.[11] In particular, they were mesmerized by class differences based upon local variations in property ownership, which they had already attacked through measures such as land reform and the socialist transformation of the economy. Then, in the post-1958 period, measures such as the shift to a brigade accounting level, the "Dazhai work point system," and the elimination of piece rates and bonuses were aimed at reducing inequalities within local communities and organizations. As a result, income differences became smaller within cities and within production teams in the countryside. For example, estimates of the Gini coefficient of income distribution within Chinese urban areas in the late 1970s range from .16 to .25, compared to figures in the range of .27 to .53 for other developing societies; several village income surveys in the same period yield similarly low figures.[12]

The major factor contributing to overall inequality in a developing society, however, is not this sort of local inequality but, rather, income differences between town and countryside and across regions within rural areas.[13] Such income differences seem to have increased after the 1950s. In regard to the rural-urban gap, if we compare the mid-1950s with the late-1970s, the gap seems to have widened considerably. One study estimates that the ratio of urban to rural incomes increased from about 2:1 to about 3:1 over this time period; another suggests that if we take into account the growing value of urban subsidies, the gap actually widened to between 5 and 6:1.[14] Research by Nicholas Lardy also documents the widening of the gap between town and country in consumption of staples such as grain, cooking oil, and cotton cloth.[15]

Why did the rural-urban gap widen despite the rhetoric and policy aimed at closing it? Several factors were involved. Urban areas witnessed not only the growing value of subsidies to urban residents but also a sharp rise in the proportion of the urban population employed, from about 30 percent in the 1950s to over 50 percent by the late 1970s. Factors affecting rural areas were underinvestment by the state in agriculture (with less than 15 percent of state investment funds expended there), bureaucratic interference in farming operations, and restrictions on migration that prevented the rural poor from moving to the cities (and, hence, sending remittances home to their relatives in the villages). Whether the millions of urbanites resettling in the villages made a net economic contribution there or became a financial burden is debatable.

Trends in regional inequality in the distribution of incomes after the 1950s are less clear, but the available evidence suggests that, in the Maoist period, disparities were not reduced and may actually have grown significantly. A number of factors may have contributed to regional income gaps. China's green revolution was concentrated in lowland areas with well-irrigated fields, and thus helped these rich areas become still richer. Bureaucratic controls over commerce prevented many rural areas from gaining access to urban markets and ensured that prosperous suburban communes would reap most of the benefits flowing from rising urban incomes. Over time, the state's grain tax system became regressive rather than progressive. The state procured a declining share of grain output and therefore had less available for redistribution to depressed areas. In fact, the authorities were noticeably reluctant to implement policies that would have redistributed resources from rich communes, counties, and provinces to poor ones, which reflected their insensitivity toward nonclass (i.e., regional) cleavages in Chinese society. In the late 1970s, some of the poorest areas were those that had achieved relative prosperity earlier by growing specialized crops but had become impoverished as a result of the "grain first" policy of the late-Mao period.[16] State price-setting and restrictive commercial policies prevented flood- and drought-stricken areas from benefiting from price rises and marketing opportunities; restrictions on migration also hurt the poorest areas most, by keeping their surplus laborers bottled up locally.

Thus, income distribution within many communities probably improved under Mao, but differences between city and countryside, and perhaps between different rural regions, increased. What the net result of these trends was for income distribution among the entire population is not clear, but my presumption is that it probably got somewhat worse, with the growing inequalities more than outweighing the factors that were becoming more equal.

Any analysis of the distribution of political power under Mao must necessarily be even more subjective. It seems fairly clear, however, at least in certain important respects, that inequality increased overall.

First, regarding the horizontal dimension of political inequality, government policy in the mid-1950s was moving toward the elimination of class labels and other markers of political status and toward the promotion of equality before the law and the state, whereas after 1962 class and political struggles were reemphasized and class labels and political "hats" increasingly affected selection for party membership, cadre posts, and other power positions. The mass stigmatization of a significant portion of the population during the struggles of the Cultural Revolution and later campaigns, and the incarceration of some of those stigmatized, clearly heightened distinctions based on relative political status. It could be argued that the intent of these efforts was compensatory—to increase the power of the disadvantaged by reducing the power of the advantaged—but, on balance, the effect was to create a giant political pecking order rather than a situation of equal political rights.

With respect to the vertical dimension of power, however, the consequences of Maoist policies are more debatable. Was not the ethos of mass participation in political campaigns responsible for reducing the distance between subjects and rulers in China? Here one must distinguish between the initial results of the Cultural Revolution and their long-run implications. Initially, powerful bureaucrats were cast into political oblivion; the party and its various "transmission belt" organizations ceased to function normally; and Cultural Revolution activists—released from organizational discipline—were able to challenge authority in ways that previously would have been unthinkable. Clearly, a major initial consequence of Maoist policies was dramatic reduction in vertical power disparities across much of Chinese society (though to a greater degree in urban areas and in civilian life than in rural areas and in the PLA).

On the other hand, the long-run consequences of the Cultural Revolution were quite the opposite. Humpty Dumpty was put back together again when the party and other control organizations were rebuilt after 1968; moreover, these organizations were reconstructed in a changed situation. The Cultural Revolution had resulted in the confiscation of much private housing in the cities, restrictions on free markets and private enterprise, extensions of rationing, elimination of the limited degree of choice that individuals had enjoyed in university and job selection, and other changes designed to create a purer socialist environment.[17] The paradoxical result was that an antibureaucratic outburst, the Cultural Revolution, produced a social order in which bureaucratic allocation of resources became more dominant and individual choice, private initiative, and market distribution were almost totally suppressed, particularly in urban areas. The participatory rhetoric that continued even after the Cultural Revolution was counterbalanced by changes that concentrated even more power in the hands of bureaucrats. In this situation mass participation within organizations became highly contrived and manipulated, as Andrew Walder has documented thoroughly in his writings on factory organization.[18] In the countryside, a somewhat comparable trend occurred as the autonomy of production teams was increasingly violated and higher bureaucratic authorities intervened more directly in the life of the villages. So, in spite of appearances, the vertical power differentials between the state authorities on the one hand and the ordinary population on the other grew during the late Mao years. Thus, in both income distribution and power distribution, relationships became more unequal in important respects in the period of Mao's "egalitarian" thrust.

Stratification in Post-Mao China

What, we might now ask, are the trends occurring in *post*-Mao China? If the Maoist rhetoric concealed trends that were in fact making China a more unequal place in which to live, might not the inegalitarian rhetoric of the Deng regime conceal growing equality? A variety of evidence does point to reduced inequality, although it is still too early, and the evidence is still too sketchy, to be conclusive.

Again, let us start by considering economic inequalities, particularly those relating to income. To some extent we can see tendencies that are the reverse of those described for the late-Mao period. It seems probable (although even on this point there is little detailed information) that income differences within communities are increasing—a trend particularly likely in rural villages, where entrepreneurial peasants have been freed to "get rich" while collective welfare measures have weakened. In the cities the picture is less clear, inasmuch as some policies that increase differentials do not benefit the most advantaged. For instance, the revival of piece rates and bonuses, and the removal in 1984 of the rule limiting bonus payments to two and one-half months' wages, primarily benefit manual workers rather than high-ranking cadres or intellectuals; in many cases, they may also work to the advantage of young and vigorous workers rather than older workers with high seniority. As one enthusiastic testimonial put it in describing the changed wage system for coal miners, "Now underground young miners can earn around 200 yuan a month. Some even can earn 300 yuan, more than a mayor!"[19] At least in some instances, then, recent changes may be helping to improve the lot of those who previously had been poorly paid, thus increasing overall equality.[20] What little evidence we have for rural areas does not point in this direction, however. A widely cited study from a county in Shanxi Province claims that most of the "specialized households" in the villages there involve former rural cadres and their families or returned soldiers and middle-school graduates—in other words, people who can be assumed to be advantaged already.[21]

With respect to the rural-urban income gap, official survey statistics claim that prosperity has increased more quickly in rural areas than in urban ones over the period 1978–1984, with real rural incomes per capita going up by 166 percent; at the same time, real urban incomes per capita increased about 92 percent.[22] Accordingly, the official estimates of the ratio of urban-to-rural incomes decreased from 2.37:1 in 1978 to 1.71:1 in 1983.[23] Official sources attribute the more rapid increase in rural areas to the combination of increases in state agricultural procurement prices in 1979 and reforms in agriculture that have generated more efficiency and higher productivity, particularly the decollectivization of farming activities and the contracting of those activities out to peasant families. However, subsidies to urbanites have also been increasing very rapidly, perhaps rapidly enough to cancel out the claimed faster rate of rural income improvement, given that the official figures on incomes do not include the value of these subsidies.[24]

In the face of these conflicting indicators, we can at least point to certain areas in which rural residents seem to be gaining on their urban brethren. The percentage of family income spent on food, an important indicator of relative living standards, declined in rural areas and, by 1984, was close to the urban rate of 58 percent.[25] In addition, the percentage of total bank savings held by rural residents rose from 26 percent in 1978 to 36 percent in 1984.[26] Although these latter statistics might be taken to indicate that peasants could not find merchandise to purchase with their increased incomes, there are indications that they are beginning to catch up with urban rates of purchase and ownership of desirable consumer durables. In 1980, 35.5 percent as many rural as urban families owned sewing machines; by 1984, the figure had risen to 54.9 percent. Regarding bicycles, the rural-urban ownership ratio increased during this same period from 29.1 percent to 45.8 percent; with respect to wristwatches, it climbed from 16.8 percent to 38.7 percent; and for radios, it rose from 39.5 percent to 59.3 percent of the urban rate. Even in regard to a newer and therefore scarcer commodity, the television set, rural ownership increased during this period from 1.2 percent to 8.5 percent of the urban level.[27] In the one area in which rural residents already had an advantage, housing space, they maintained or slightly increased that advantage from 1978 to 1983, even though they had to finance new housing themselves; meanwhile, urbanites benefited from a boom in the construction of state housing.[28] In sum, a variety of factors indicate that the trend toward a widening of the rural-urban gap has been arrested and that the gap may even be narrowing in significant respects.

On the question of trends affecting regional income differences in rural areas in the post-Mao period, the evidence is inconclusive. Authorities in China deny that polarization is taking place and present data to show a general increase in incomes of the rural population. But, to date, the data released are not sufficient to determine whether regional income disparities are growing. Nevertheless, several changes have occurred that may work in favor of greater equality. First, the reduction of state interference in farming and the repudiation of the "grain first" policy has allowed some depressed areas, such as the traditional cotton growing areas of Shandong Province, to resume cultivation of their specialties and thus increase their incomes with unusual speed. Second, insofar as the adoption of the household contracting system has been an important contributor to the increase in rural incomes (an issue on which there is still some debate), it appears that this system was adopted first in relatively poor locales and provinces, and only later—and often reluctantly—in more prosperous areas. In other words, in contrast to the effects of the green revolution of the 1960s, decollectivization was an income-enhancing change that benefited poor areas before rich ones (although rich areas may now be making up for lost time).

In addition, the loosening in 1984 of migration rules, which permitted some peasants to relocate in towns and cities and even to get permanent nonagricultural registrations in small towns, as well as measures that encourage rural families to specialize in nonagricultural pursuits, may provide options that will make it easier for depressed areas to reduce their populations and to benefit from a flow of remittances from the nonagricultural sector. (The question remains, however, as to whether people in depressed areas are more likely than those in prosperous villages near cities to take advantage of these new opportunities; therefore, the consequences of these changes for regional income distribution remain uncertain.) The increasing share of agricultural production that is exchanged on the market at negotiated prices, as a result of the relaxation of state control of trade in key commodities, may mean that prices will rise to reflect scarcity and fall when goods are abundant, thus helping to correct for local disparities. Finally, although state investment in agriculture has in fact fallen since 1978, special state policies have been adopted to deal with the problems of poverty-stricken regions—including reductions of agricultural taxes, special food distributions, and increased state investment in local road construction and other forms of rural infrastructure.

Whether these various steps together are enough to compensate for opposing tendencies, such as the spin-off effects in wealthy suburban areas of the opening of more cities to foreign investment and new urban growth, we will not know until detailed rural income distribution figures are released. The point to be stressed here is simply this: It is not obvious that post-Mao trends are increasing regional income inequalities in the countryside, given the existence of contrary policies and indications whose net effect is not known. It is at least possible that regional inequalities in incomes have been reduced, even if local income inequalities are increasing.[29]

With respect to overall income-distribution trends in China, the picture seems to be mixed. We have speculated that local inequalities are increasing and that the rural-urban gap may be narrowing somewhat, with regional trends in rural areas still unclear. But to the extent that some portion of the peasantry is succeeding in "getting rich," this is a positive development, even if many urbanites are becoming irate about the "violation" of the "natural order of things." The gap between rural and urban incomes in China had by the late 1970s become quite large in comparison with other Asian developing societies.[30] Judgments about equality and inequality depend not only on what is happening to the overall income distribution but also on whether those who have been disadvantaged before are now benefiting—and the envy-stimulating prosperity of some peasants seems to indicate success in this regard. Having an increasing number of peasants who bridge the rural-urban income gap should help to reduce a major source of overall inequality.

However skeptical we may be of the Deng regime's argument that inequality will lead to a prosperity that, in turn, will eventually "trickle down" to the disadvantaged, we should be aware that considerable cross-national evidence exists in support of such a sequence of events.[31] As economic development proceeds and more people move out of agriculture into a wide range of nonagricultural pursuits, inequalities of income do tend to get smaller, in both socialist and capitalist countries. There are various grounds, then, on which we might be cautiously optimistic in our projection that current policies will not lead to increasing differences in income distribution.

Complex trends are also occurring in the realm of power distribution, but there, too, some changes indicate greater equality rather than inequality. With respect to the horizontal dimension of political status, some 20 million individuals have had "bad class" labels removed, political victims of earlier campaigns have been rehabilitated, and political struggle campaigns have been declared unnecessary. (On the other hand, of course, some "Gang of Four elements" and members of other new outcast categories have been penalized; some have been arrested and even executed. But it would appear that those losing their political rights are fewer in number than those regaining such rights, although we lack adequate evidence to prove that this is the case.) The development of a formal legal system and the resurrection of the legal profession are presumed to provide greater equality to all citizens before the law than did the "mass justice" of the Cultural Revolution period, and special disciplinary inspection commissions and press publicity have focused attention on the major problem of trying to keep high-ranking cadres and their families from acting as if they were above the law. The separate and inferior status of peasants relative to urbanites has been at least partially ameliorated. Changes in the system restricting migration allow and even encourage peasants to come into some towns, thereby permitting them to change from agricultural to nonagricultural household registrations if they secure nonagricultural employment there.[32] In 1984, a nationwide system of identity cards was introduced; it replaced an arrangement under which urbanites, but not peasants, carried personal identity documents. It is worth noting, also, that the separate status of national minority groups has been modified, at least to the extent that they are increasingly subject to family planning regulations, whereas previously these regulations had applied only to the Han Chinese.

To be sure, some contrary tendencies have occurred as well, such as the revival of special privileges for Overseas Chinese, returned students, and a variety of specialists and experts.[33] Still, on balance, the post-Mao era seems to have weakened political status distinctions and produced a greater stress on the equality of all citizens before the state.

In the vertical dimension of political power inequality, signs of clear improvement are evident, although the magnitude of the changes to date has been modest. The election of National People's Congress (NPC) delegates, establishment of limits on terms of office, and creation of disciplinary inspection commissions do not, of course, fundamentally alter the monopoly of power held by the CCP and its bureaucratic appendages; moreover, there are as many signs now as in the Mao period that bureaucrats sternly resist attempts to limit their power and privileges. Nevertheless, some reforms have, indeed, given the ordinary population more options and more autonomy.

These improvements in options and autonomy are particularly visible in the countryside, where the decollectivization of farming activity has reduced the power of local officials, thus enabling peasant families to reclaim some of the power over decisions affecting their lives that they lost in the mid-1950s. However, even in the cities, ordinary people have gained with respect to bureaucracy. They have more choice regarding schools and jobs; more goods are available without ration coupons or "going through channels"; and leisure time activities are not as regimented as in the past. Legal protections are still very weak, but individuals are less totally dependent upon their bureaucratic overseers than they were in the late-Mao era. Ordinary citizens may not find themselves in a better position to criticize and force changes upon their superiors, but they are somewhat more able to ignore their bosses and go their own ways. The overall result has been some reduction in vertical power differentiation.

Much of Deng's reform program, of course, is concerned precisely with improving productivity and efficiency by reducing bureaucratic centralization, making somewhat greater use of market exchanges, and encouraging local initiative and individual choice. Some statements made by Deng and his entourage give the impression that they are willing even to question the fundamental tenets of their Leninist political system. In a speech in 1980, for example, Liao Gailong, one of Deng's close advisers on ideological issues, was quite blunt about what was wrong with China's organizational system. In particular, he charged that

> Lenin's political theory neglected the democratic aspect of proletarian dictatorship, but attached too much importance to the aspect of violent suppression. He even said that proletarian dictatorship was "iron" dictatorship not bound by any laws. . . . This dictatorship over-emphasized the role of force and emphasized the role of not being bound by anything. Thus, the power of the party and the state became over-centralized in the hands of the Central Committee of the Communist Party and finally became over-centralized in the hands of one or a few leaders. . . . Thus, over a long period of time, it seemed to us that socialism was centralism, a high degree of centralism; that the concentration of power in the hands of a party central committee and then in the hands of leaders was socialism.[34]

Liao's prescription specified reforms aimed at reducing this over-concentration of power. The implication might be drawn that Deng and his advisers understand the political consequences of their economic reforms—that they require, and will further foster, a weakening of the concentration of power that previously existed (which I have termed vertical power inequality). One can raise questions about how much support there is within the CCP leadership for the sort of blunt analysis given by Liao (which closely followed comparable statements made by Deng himself in 1980). Some analysts would also note that such direct challenges to the CCP's Leninist legacy have not been voiced since 1980. Still, the fact remains that the thrust of the reforms currently being implemented is to weaken the heretofore nearly total subordination of individuals to their bureaucratic superiors.

Conclusions

The perhaps novel argument advanced here is that the Maoist era was not really so egalitarian, and the current regime not so inegalitarian, as many have assumed. This is not to imply that China today is a highly egalitarian society or even that it is well on the way to becoming one. Not all of the post-Mao policies and trends are working to promote equality. In addition to the apparent increases in inequalities in local communities, there are other developments that seem to point toward growing disparities. Witness, for example, the substantial amount of anecdotal evidence that in both rural and urban areas many cadres are doing what they can to take advantage of new policies to enrich themselves rather than their disadvantaged neighbors. Note, also, the absolute decline in secondary-school enrollments, particularly in rural areas—a decline that seems likely to make it more difficult than in the past for rural residents to compete for those privileged positions requiring substantial education.

But such indicators do not really undermine the primary argument, which is intended to challenge some prevalent assumptions about social life under Mao and at present. Although many analysts have believed that equality was being promoted vigorously under Mao, in fact certain kinds of systemic inequalities were growing, and in important ways China was a much more unequal place when Mao died in 1976 than it had been two decades earlier, before Mao led his nation off on a quest for the socialist holy grail. If the reality under Mao did not match appearances, might that also be true today? Underneath the rhetoric that seems to indicate growing inequality in Deng's China, there is evidence that in a number of specific areas inequalities seem to be getting smaller. More data are clearly needed on many of the points raised here, but it would be misleading to look primarily at trends within particular communities or factories, where such data may be most readily available, and to ignore the trends in society at large, which may point in a quite different direction. In the late-Mao period, local inequalities were to some extent being reduced, but perhaps at the expense of increasing cross-community differences. One should at least entertain the hypothesis, with respect to the post-Mao period, that local inequalities may be increasing while the overall level of inequality in China is declining.

Underlying the "widely held but mistaken" view being criticized here are two basic assumptions. The first is that economic development inevitably conflicts with the pursuit of equality, so that one has to be sacrificed if the other is to be achieved. Although such a trade-off appears to have occurred in many countries, particularly during the early stages of their development,[35] in actual fact this may not always be the case. Rather, differing strategies for development may have varying implications for equality and inequality. In some cases, particularly those of Taiwan and to some extent South Korea, rapid development has not been accompanied by increased inequality; indeed, it may even have led to increased equality.[36] One might hypothesize that an agriculture-oriented, labor-intensive, and export-promoting strategy of development is more likely to spread the benefits of growth over a broad range than the sort of urban-oriented, capital-intensive, autarkic path that has characterized Soviet-style development. Thus, the effort of leaders under Deng to switch away from such a Soviet-style strategy may, in fact, be an effort to combine growth with equality, rather than to sacrifice the one for the other.

The second basic assumption challenged here is the idea that market mechanisms inevitably foster inequalities, which can be effectively countered only through the kind of state redistribution that is possible under socialism. Recent research on Eastern Europe suggests that this assumption is invalid on two counts. First, market relationships do not inevitably foster inequality. Second, state redistribution does not always foster equality. In Eastern Europe it is quite clear from research by Ivan Szelenyi that state redistribution has often resulted in the allotment of funds and resources not to the poor but to those who are already advantaged—to bureaucrats, intellectuals, and, to a lesser extent, urbanites in general.[37] In this set of circumstances, as Szelenyi has suggested, market reforms may help foster equality by making available to the poor such commodities as housing, health care, consumer durables, and other scarce resources that would otherwise be monopolized by those higher in the bureaucratic pecking (and allocation) order. This insightful analysis may also be applicable to China.

Market-oriented reforms may not, in some circumstances, promote inequality, but may instead help correct some inequalities fostered by a bureaucratic distribution system. From this one might conclude that the most desirable system would be some sort of mixed economy, in which market distribution would help correct for inequalities fostered by bureaucratic allocation and bureaucratic allocation would help correct for inequalities fostered by market distribution. However, Szelenyi and his collaborators have recently argued that the matter is more complex than this simple solution would imply, and that some kinds of market distribution may reinforce, rather than correct for, inequalities produced by the socialist distribution system.[38]

The crucial issue, then, would seem to be whether the introduction of market-oriented reforms enables those already advantaged by the state allocation system to increasingly monopolize the new opportunities made available via the market, or whether those benefits will in large measure work to the advantage of those who were benefiting less from the state allocation system.

In short, analyzing the implications of the reforms in China is no easy matter. Enough evidence and arguments have been presented here to raise doubts about whether the current rhetoric in favor of inegalitarian values and the replacement of state allocation with market distribution in some areas mean that the reforms are producing a "triumph of inequality." Whether the tendencies that promote equality or those that promote inequality will win out in the long run remains an open question, however. In the current scene, we can see both school drop-outs who prosper by setting up new restaurants and state cadres who set up their own (theoretically illegal) family enterprises and use their contacts to get business and favors. We can see peasants fleeing poverty-stricken villages and getting jobs in new town factories, but we can also see the party secretaries of rich suburban communes appointing their nephews to run enterprises that get lucrative contracts from urban industries.

The balance of the benefits resulting from the new rules of the game still remains to be determined. The conclusion, then, is not that everything is becoming more equal under Deng, but only that one cannot simply *assume* that everything is becoming more unequal. Instead, we need to discover much more about what is happening and who is benefiting, and to examine what we find with a precise mental and moral calculus. Only then will we be able to judge whether the current reforms are leading China toward a more or less egalitarian future.[39]

Notes

1. William Mills, "Generational Change in China," *Problems of Communism* 32, no. 6 (November-December 1983), p. 17.

2. I should note, in all candor, that I have stressed this misguided view in some of my own previous writings. See, in particular, Martin King Whyte, "Destratification and Restratification in China," in G. Berreman (ed.), *Social Inequality: Comparative and Developmental Approaches* (New York: Academic Press, 1981).

3. See, for example, Alexander Eckstein, *China's Economic Revolution* (Cambridge, England: Cambridge University Press, 1977), pp. 303–304.

4. During the earlier radical upsurge of the Great Leap Forward, Zhang Chunqiao wrote an article advocating elimination of the wage system and a return to the "supply system" used to pay cadres before 1949; then, after the idea was revived in 1974, Mao was annoyed when the Ministry of Finance told him it would not work. See Liao Gailong, "Historical Experiences and Our Road to Development," *Issues and Studies* 17, no. 11 (November 1981), pp. 89–90.

5. See Susan Shirk, "The Decline of Virtuocracy in China," in James L. Watson (ed.), *Class and Social Stratification in Post-Revolution China* (Cambridge, England: Cambridge University Press, 1984).

6. *Foreign Broadcast Information Service, Daily Report: People's Republic of China* (hereafter *FBIS-CHI*), October 1, 1984, p. P1.

7. *FBIS-CHI*, October 3, 1984, p. S3.

8. For a convenient summary of major indices of inequality, see H. Alker, Jr., and B. Russett, "Indices for Comparing Inequality," in R. Merritt and S. Rokkan (eds.), *Comparing Nations* (New Haven, Conn.: Yale University Press, 1966).

9. The Gini coefficient is a measure of the extent to which the cumulative income distribution curve (the "Lorenz curve") deviates from the 45° angle line that would indicate total equality of incomes in the population. As such, the Gini coefficient can take values from 0 to 1, and a lower value indicates greater equality. See the discussion and illustrations in Alker and Russett, "Indices for Comparing Inequality."

10. The first part of the comparison concerns "late-Mao China," roughly the period 1958–1976. The baseline thus concerns the conditions of the mid-1950s rather than those that existed prior to 1949. This choice is deliberate, as it is not the gains (or losses) of the revolution that are being assessed but, rather, the consequences of the distinctive policies followed after 1957.

11. Mao's insensitivity to these other dimensions is somewhat puzzling given that, in a number of his statements in the 1950s (particularly in "On the Correct Handling of Contradictions Among the People"), he set forth an unorthodox view that stressed cleavages other than those based on property ownership.

12. For urban areas, see M. Whyte and W. Parish, *Urban Life in Contemporary China* (Chicago: University of Chicago Press, 1984), p. 44; and World Bank, *China: Socialist Economic Development—The Main Report* (Washington, D.C.: World Bank, 1981), Table 3.17. For rural areas, consult M. Blecher, "Income Distribution in Small Rural Communities," *China Quarterly*, no. 68 (December 1976), pp. 805–811; and M. Selden, "Income and Inequality in a Model

Village," unpublished paper (1981). Blecher, for one, argues that village income distributions were more equal in the 1970s than in the 1950s and 1960s.

13. In this connection, the reader might note the claim by one authority that about 25 percent of the overall income disparities in rural China in the 1930s were attributable to class differences within villages, with the remaining 75 percent due to regional variation. See Charles Roll, "Incentives and Motivation in China: The 'Reality' of Rural Inequality" (unpublished and undated), p. 29.

14. See W. Parish, "Egalitarianism in Chinese Society," *Problems of Communism* 29, no. 1 (January-February 1981), pp. 37–53; and T. Rawski, "The Simple Arithmetic of Chinese Income Distribution," *Keizai Kenkyu* 33, no. 1 (1982), pp. 12–26.

15. Nicholas Lardy, *Agriculture in China's Modern Economic Development* (Cambridge, England: Cambridge University Press, 1983), pp. 157–159.

16. For documentation of the cases of Shandong cotton-growing counties and other regions, see Lardy, *Agriculture.* For somewhat similar judgments about trends in this period, see D. Perkins and S. Yusuf, *Rural Development in China* (Baltimore: Johns Hopkins University Press, 1984), ch. 6.

17. This theme is discussed in detail in Whyte and Parish, *Urban Life in Contemporary China.*

18. See, in particular, Andrew Walder, "Organized Dependency and Cultures of Authority in Chinese Industry," *Journal of Asian Studies* 43, no. 11 (November 1983), pp. 51–76.

19. Quoted in Jing Wei, "Miners' Past and Present," *Beijing Review* 28, no. 10 (March 11, 1985), p. 21.

20. In fact, data released after this paper was written indicate that the urban income distribution improved from Gini = .23 in 1977 to Gini = .17 in 1984. See Li Chengrui, "Economic Reform Brings Better Life," *Beijing Review* 28, no. 29, pp. 21–22. (The figures were recalculated by the present author from the data provided.)

21. See the translation of the details of this survey in *FBIS-CHI*, January 25, 1984, p. K4ff.

22. See Li, "Economic Reform," p. 18.

23. Ibid.

24. See Nicholas Lardy, "Consumption and Living Standards in China, 1978–83," *China Quarterly*, no. 100 (December 1984), p. 863.

25. It has been claimed that the rural rate was 67.7 percent in 1978 and 59.0 percent in 1984. See Li, "Economic Reform," p. 18.

26. Ibid., p. 20.

27. These percentages were computed from figures in ibid., p. 19.

28. According to official survey statistics, peasant housing space per capita increased by 43 percent over the five-year period, whereas urban housing space increased 40 percent. See *Beijing Review* 27, no. 42 (October 15, 1984), p. 30.

29. My initial effort to manipulate the crude published data on rural income distributions indicated a decline in the Gini index, and thus heightened

equality, after 1978. More detailed figures released after this paper was written and covering a longer time period indicate a slight *increase* in the Gini coefficient from .25 in 1978 to .28 in 1984. (See Li, "Economic Reform," pp. 20–22. I recalculated the figures from the data provided.) However, since these are overall figures that combine regional and local effects, one still cannot be certain as to whether regional inequalities are increasing, decreasing, or remaining more or less constant.

30. For limited estimates pertaining to other Asian countries, with urban-rural income ratios in the range from 1.14 to 2.7, see Michael Lipton, *Why Poor People Stay Poor* (Cambridge, Mass.: Harvard University Press, 1976), p. 430.

31. See, for example, F. Paukert, "Income Distribution and Different Levels of Development: A Review of the Evidence," *International Labour Review* 108, nos. 2–3, pp. 97–125.

32. This modification applies only to towns below the county-seat level, and even in these cases, the new nonagriculturalists are apparently not entitled to urban grain rations. Still, the modification is a foot in the urban door.

33. For example, such groups are now favored in such realms as recruitment into the CCP, access to new housing, and ability to have an "above-quota" child.

34. Liao, "Historical Experiences," p. 93.

35. Again, see the evidence reviewed in Paukert, "Income Distribution," pp. 97–125.

36. See, for example, J. Fei, G. Ranis, and S. Kuo, *Growth with Equity: The Taiwan Case* (New York: Oxford University Press, 1979).

37. See the impressive documentation of this argument by Ivan Szelenyi in his book, *Urban Inequalities Under State Socialism* (New York: Oxford University Press, 1983).

38. See R. Manchin and I. Szelenyi, "Social Policy Under State Socialism: Market, Redistribution, and Social Inequalities in East European Socialist Societies," in G. Esping-Anderson, L. Rainwater, and M. Rein (eds.), *Comparative Social Policies* (Armonk, N.Y.: M. E. Sharpe, forthcoming).

39. I have not addressed the "so what" issue here: Does the extent or type of inequality have any important consequences, in terms of such matters as political conflict or social problems? On this point I would say that equality is of greatest concern to the outside observer. For the members of any society, what matters most is not equality per se, but equity—that is, whether people are perceived as getting what is due them, and whether existing inequalities are seen as just and fair. For some thoughts on the equity issue, see Martin King Whyte, "The Politics of Life Chances in the People's Republic of China," in Yu-ming Shaw (ed.), *Power and Policy in the PRC* (Boulder, Colo.: Westview Press, 1985).

About the Contributors

A. Doak Barnett is Professor of Chinese Studies at the School of Advanced International Studies, The Johns Hopkins University. He is the author of numerous books on China, including *China on the Eve of Communist Takeover* (Westview, 1985); *The Making of Foreign Policy in China* (Westview, 1985); *China After Mao; Cadres, Bureaucracy, and Political Power in Communist China; Uncertain Passage: China's Transition to the Post-Mao Era; China and the Major Powers in East Asia;* and *China's Economy in Global Perspective.*

Ralph N. Clough is Coordinator of the SAIS China Forum at the School of Advanced International Studies, The Johns Hopkins University. A retired Foreign Service Officer who was director for Chinese Affairs in the Department of State, he is the author of *East Asia and U.S. Security* and *Island China.*

Paul H.B. Godwin is Associate Professor of Asian Studies at the Air University, Maxwell Air Force Base. He edited *The Chinese Defense Establishment* (Westview, 1983) and is a contributor to *Chinese Defense Policy* and *China and the World.* His articles have appeared in several journals.

Harry Harding, a Senior Fellow in the Foreign Policy Studies Program at the Brookings Institution, is currently studying the reforms under way in post-Mao China and international relations in Northeast Asia. He is the editor of *China's Foreign Relations in the 1980s* and the author of *Organizing China: The Problem of Bureaucracy, 1949–1976* and of other works on China's domestic and foreign affairs.

Perry Link is Professor of Chinese at UCLA, with a specialization in modern Chinese literature, society, and popular culture. He has written *Mandarin Ducks and Butterflies,* which concerns popular fiction in early twentieth-century China, and has edited three anthologies of post-Mao literature.

Dwight H. Perkins is concurrently Director of the Harvard Institute for International Development and Harold Hitchings Burbank Professor of Political Economy. He is the author, coauthor, or editor of nine books and more than fifty articles, most of which deal with the economic development of China, Korea, and other parts of Asia.

Martin King Whyte is Professor of Sociology at the University of Michigan, with a specialization in the comparative institutional development of the Soviet Union and China. He is the author of *Small Groups and Political Rituals in China* and coauthor of *Village and Family in Contemporary China* and *Urban Life in Contemporary China.* He has also written approximately fifty journal articles on China and Russia.

Index

DUE DATE